WINDOW GARDENING

DEVOTED SPECIALLY TO

THE CULTURE OF FLOWERS

AND

ORNAMENTAL PLANTS,

FOR

In Door Use and Parlor Decoration

Edited by

HENRY T. WILLIAMS

with a new introduction by

H. PETER LOEWER

WALKER & COMPANY
NEW YORK

Introduction copyright © 1976 by H. Peter Loewer

All rights reserved. No part of this book may be reproduced or transmitted in any form or by any means, electric or mechanical, including photocopying, recording, or by any information storage and retrieval system, without permission in writing from the Publisher.

This edition first published in the United States of America in 1976 by the Walker Publishing Company, Inc.

Published simultaneously in Canada by Fitzhenry & Whiteside, Limited, Toronto.

ISBN: 0-8027-7104-1

Library of Congress Catalog Card Number: 76-25743

Printed in the United States of America.

10 9 8 7 6 5 4 3 2 1

INTRODUCTION

One hundred and five years have passed since the initial publication of *Window Gardening*. Unlike so many instructional tomes of yesteryear, whose only attraction is a bit of nostalgia, this volume remains a unique gathering of imaginative approaches to indoor gardening together with some great ideas for hanging baskets. My wife struggled for three nights, weaving a basket of freshly dug rose roots (as suggested on page 101). She admits that it wasn't easy, but the result is a classic Victorian container festooned with fuscia that now graces our front porch.

A few things have changed over the years. The ease of applying modern fertilizers allows us to skip the uses of quano water (chapter three). Quassia wood solution is no longer available for pest control. The "carnation twitter," as a name for the infamous spider mite, has long since been replaced with invectives of a more startling nature (chapter five). We know that "damping-off" of emergent seedlings is caused by a fungus, not water-logged plant tissues, but the author was correct about too much water being disastrous for seedlings (chapter six). Hot frames, or seed beds, need no longer be heated with kerosene lamps, with the advent of thermostatically controlled electric cables.

A glance at the picture list on pages 84-88 shows the amazing variety of plant life available to our Victorian ancestors, and, except for a few changes in Latin nomenclature, it is today as good a list of useful house plants as the day it first appeared. In fact most of the advice given in the following pages can be profitably followed by the modern gardener. The instructions for cyclamen (page 151) are, for example, correct, unlike most of today's gardening books.

The Ladies' Floral Cabinet Company and Mr. Henry T. Williams are to be gratefully remembered for their initial publication of this volume in 1871, and Walker and Company happily thanked for reprinting it in 1976. It is sincerely hoped that today's readers will be as amused and instructed as I was.

H. Peter Loewer

Cochecton Center, N.Y.
June, 1976

INDEX.

PART I.

CHAPTER		PAGES
I.	Window Gardening: Its Pleasures—Increase in Popular Taste—Refining Influences..	5 to 10
II.	Location and Designs for Window Gardens..	11 to 22
III.	General Management of Window Gardens..	23 to 35
IV.	Special Care of Window Gardens in Winter, Spring, Summer, Autumn.......	36 to 44
V.	Insects, and how to kill them..	45 to 48
VI.	Propagation from Seeds, Cuttings, &c...	49 to 52
VII.	Propagating Boxes, Heating Cases and Cold Frames............................	53 to 56
VIII.	Window Pots, Boxes, Jardinieres and Plant Stands...............................	57 to 76
IX.	Conservatories and Greenhouses...	77 to 90

PART II.

PLANTS FOR WINDOW GARDENS.

CHAPTER		
X.	Hanging Baskets...	91 to 110
XI.	The Ivy for Decorative purposes...	111 to 118
XII.	Climbing Vines—Balcony Gardening...	119 to 137
XIII.	Bulbs..	138 to 157
XIV.	Ferneries, Wardian Cases, and Fern Decorations..............................	158 to 188

PREFACE

THE taste for Window Gardening and the plant decoration of apartments is becoming universal; scarcely a cottage or villa but has its attempts, whether simple or elaborate, to decorate the windows, the porch, or the balcony with some few flower-pots or climbing vines; it is a sign of healthy sentiment, for the presence of flowers always aids in the development of refinement and an elevated taste.

This volume has been written specially as a help and an encouragement to ladies and all flower-lovers, to assist them with judicious hints and suggestions in their efforts to make home more beautiful by the use of plants around their windows or balconies.

With the exception of a very few pages, properly credited to English writers (Mr. Robinson and Shirley Hibberd, upon subjects as yet unfamiliar to American readers), the literary matter of this volume is entirely original, being contributed by the Editor, and assisted by several American writers, enthusiastic flower lovers, who have cheerfully written articles on special topics.

The aim has been to produce a volume suited to American uses, which would be simple, reliable, adapted to the needs of amateurs and beginners in home plant culture, yet abundant in suggestions of the many ways to render home attractive.

Previous editions of this volume have been called for rapidly, and received with marked pleasure, and it is hoped that, in this new edition, where the errors of former editions have been corrected, the reader will still continue to show favor toward a work issued rather for the public good than the personal emolument of the author.

Should the interested reader feel pleased with this little testimonial to one of the most beautiful of all departments of flower culture, and the desire of the author to foster the fancy for window ornament, he will not regret his effort to add some definite encouragement to the more extensive development of rural taste.

THE EDITOR.

Fig. 1.—Decorative Bird Cage and Flower Stand.

WINDOW GARDENING.

CHAPTER I.

Its Pleasures — Increase in Popular Taste — Refining Influences.

No home of taste is now considered complete without its Window Garden. Indeed it may be said that Window Gardening is one of the most elegant, satisfactory, yet least expensive of all departments of Rural Taste. As a useful means for developing a taste for plant-life and a love for flowers, I count nothing so effective as this simple style of gardening; for who has not noticed that where flowers reign, grace of mind and manner soon follow. One of the advantages of Window Gardening is its *simplicity*, open to every one and impossible to none. Thousands of persons confined to their homes for the greater part of their life have no greater rural estate than that which the Window Garden affords. To watch the unfolding leaves and budding flowers, the development of branch after branch, is a study of the reality of plant-life, exquisitely interesting to the soul who finds in it its only world of pleasure and sentiment.

It is a form of gardening too, of *permanent use and value*. The Window Garden is independent to a large degree of the varying seasons, for it can be made attractive every month in the year. The advent of Spring, Summer and Autumn, only render the plants of the Window Garden more luxuriant and make the flowers more brilliant, but they do not die with the first frost or cold wind in winter When the prospect without is dreary, we can still look to our fern-cases or window-boxes or hanging-baskets and behold in them objects of increased admiration, because they are so charming in their contrast with the desolateness without, and are genial remembrances of greener days gone by.

The universal popularity of Window Gardens, whether large or small, simple or elaborate, is the evidence of a growing taste for flowers and ornamental plants in all circles of society. We have only to notice in all our large cities, towns and villages, how frequent window decorations have become, sometimes seeming as if not a single house was without them in many of our most fashionable avenues. In European cities the citizens indulge even more extensively and passionately in their plant pleasures than we do; every home is decorated from the workingman's window, and its few flower-pots of balsams, to the fernery and tile jardinieres of the aristocratic mansion.

In Brussels, says M Victor Paquet, "the balconies are turned into greenhouses and miniature stoves, gay with the brightest and greenest foliage. And in Paris there are many contrivances in use by means of which the rarest and most beautiful plants are produced. Passifloras cling to columns in the upper floors; water plants start into blossom in tiny basins curiously contrived in solid brickwork, and limpid water flows down a miniature rockery from whose crevices start up ferns and lycopodiums."

The rooms of the Parisian are gay with flowers replaced freshly every day, and in the denser parts of London, black with its smoky atmosphere, may be found some of the choicest of plant-cases. An English writer visiting such a locality once was ushered into a room where the darkness was almost felt, but every window was occupied with a plant-case in which plants were growing in an astonishing manner. Ferns of the greenest and freshest hue, orchids never surpassed, were there in redolent health and vigor. He was told to his great surprise that the cases were hermetically sealed, and that no water had been administered for months

There is a never-failing charm, too, in the outside decorations of the house or Window Garden. The trellis-work of the balcony may be made ornamental with green foliage and its homeliness tastefully hidden The ivy will cover the unpainted wall and make it still more artistic. The verandah can be soon covered with the most luxuriant of profuse blooming creepers. Unsightly objects, bare gardens, and plain fences can all be relieved. In fact no home is devoid of the means of tasteful decoration. And so many and easy are the forms of window embellishments at the present day, that we know of no better device for increasing the elegancies and attractions of indoor life.

Window Gardens, too, are *educators of taste*. In our large cities it is noticeable that the fair occupants of the wealthier homes are themselves practically interested in window ornament. It is quite the fashion for their own hands to fill with pretty plants, of their own arrangement, jardinieres of costly tile, or else place them in baskets of rustic yet most artistic make After a little time when they have grown to appropriate height, or the drooping plants have attained sufficient length, the full beauty of the Window Garden is apparent. Visitors are entranced with their wondrous beauty and are free with their exclamations of delight. The passer-by on the sidewalk stops for a moment to look lovingly upon the cozy bower of bloom just inside the glazed window pane. When passing away, he still keeps it in mind, and long afterwards cherishes the memory of this artistic beauty spot. Flowers and plants, by their beauty and fragrance, are always in harmony with rich and costly furniture, pictures or statuary.

A simple flower stand near the window, a hanging basket over head, all shedding their perfume, add day by day brightness to the other genialities of the home; and all through the wintry months, furnish food for pleasant thoughts; a single plant of the Ivy trained on the wall, or festooned over the window, is a joy to all beholders

Flowers, plants too, often supply the place of children in bereaved homes; for their soul-refreshing, heart-inspiring, and eye-brightening influences, are joys to wean the thoughts from pain or sorrow.

Some mother perhaps cherishes fondly in her home a few beautiful Fuchsias placed on a stand upon the window sill She never tires of looking upon their graceful shapes, or the brightly colored jewel blossoms drooping downwards, for they remind her of the delight they once gave her little child before it went to its angel home The value to her of these treasures, with their brilliant colors and snowy waxen petals, rose-colored or purple corollas, cannot be measured with the ordinary expression of language

Among the most gratifying signs of floral taste, is the evidence of their introduction into *school rooms*. The teacher is perhaps fond of them and knows their influence. Their very delicacy, forbidding rough handling, serves to impose a wholesome restraint upon the children; if ever they are tired with their study, a few glances at the windowsill, and its pots of bloom, wreathe their faces with genial smiles, and they go to work again with willing hearts and refreshed thoughts. The curiosity of children, too, is proverbial, and many a girl learns more of nature from the living specimens before her, than from the dry details of her book of botany

Not less important can we consider flowers and plants, as the best and most practical educators of *healthy sentiment*. They are always suggestive of purity and refinement. Nothing is so conducive to cheerfulness, or creates efforts to make home attractive, like their presence in the household. Constant associations with such objects of floral beauty, fits people to rank high as useful members of society. A floral writer has already expressed these sentiments in a most charming manner .

" They are a spring of sunshine, a constant pleasure. We would have flowers in every home, for their sunny light, for their cheerful teachings, for their insensibly ennobling influence."

As an *amusement* for the *invalid,* Window Gardening through the form of plant cases, is very appropriate. We call to mind an instance of one compelled in consequence of a bodily infirmity, to take up a residence in the city.

He had enjoyed for a long time in the country the pleasures of the green-house, and endeavored whilst in the city to replace it once more. A small but inexpensive three light green-house was erected in the back yard, open, airy. There he gratified his taste for floricultural subjects by gathering together an interesting collection of valuable ferns and orchids. In an upper room was arranged a capacious fern case, and there the invalid would spend many days during the winter recumbent upon the sofa dilating upon the pleasures of being able to watch the growth of a vigorous intertwining mass of curious forms of foreign ferns, many of them productions from distant portions of the globe, New Zealand, India, Mexico, Japan

In our country homes, how common to see the plant stand before the window with its dozen or so pots of Geraniums, Primroses, Azaleas, &c., while an inva lid sister or mother reclines in the easy chair, watching it for hours with delight, unmindful of the snow driving past the window pane.

The refining influence of the flowers is no where more apparent than in our humble cottage homes; for there it is the young maiden cherishes her few pet flowers, with a deeper affection and truer love than even the skilled gardener. There is something so attractive in their very looks that none can resist their sweet and winning influence. Perhaps it may be because so few are disappointed in them, or expect them to yield a measured commercial profit. So no one's enthusiasm is gauged by dollars and cents.

In some of the strangest of conditions, there is often the most delightful display of floral bloom; the prairie log cabin may often contain a flourishing window garden, with as choice specimens as that of the rich amateur.

Few are so poor but they can find room for a few boxes and pots to grow plants and beguile the long winter hours. They should be in the window of every sitting room, in every school-house, that children, as well as parents, may be educated to the appreciation of their beauties, and their taste more readily cultivated and encouraged.

The *effects of window gardening* become more clearly seen each succeeding year. Many who have not the slightest idea of how a plant grows will obtain from the florist a simple basket of Ivy. Once living, it needs little further attention; yet the eye of the proprietor often wanders upward to it, and as the tendrils reach out, twining around the basket, upward or downward, his senses are gradually interested, and in time other plants follow, who in turn are studied. These tempt others, mere visitors, to try the same experiment, and so the contagious enthusiasm for flowers steadily spreads. In every state the love for flowers and plants is on the increase. The business of our florists is three times larger than five years ago. Our cottagers are devoting more time to the ornamentation of door yards with these floral gems, and the window sill of many a cot has its sugar bowl or cracked tea pot, doing duty for a flower pot, while we have often seen the discarded fruit can, in some wayside ranchman's cabin in the interior of the Rocky Mountains, blooming with balsams or portulacca. All classes respond to but one sentiment, "FLOWERS, GIVE US FLOWERS."

Beside the delights of window gardening in opening new resources of amusement, recreation and instruction, which nothing else can give to the home circle, is the added advantage that it is *easy;* but *very little time is required for their culture.* Some window gardens are elaborate, expensive, and are suited only for those of scientific taste, but by far the most successful are those in our every day homes, with the simplest of flowering plants. There are many more easy plans for house gardening than difficult ones. The little physical exercise needed, is a relief to mental pursuits, and a variety to domestic duties, while the daily growth of each plant and flower, which constitutes the chief delight of the young florist, and the beauty and elegance of his little garden, form a crowning gratification for his well spent hours, and stimulate an honest and desirable pride.

In some of the poorest quarters of London there may be found at any time handsomer Balsams than any professional ever raised, while some of the finest new Chrysanthemums ever produced it is said have originated in the window garden of some of these humble citizens.

A quaint old English writer calls this form of home pleasure, "*Fenestral Gardening*," (*Hortus Fenestralis*) expressive of the decoration of rooms with green drapery from the garden. Many are deterred from the commencement of a window garden, or the care for cases of plants, on account of the supposed *trouble*.

There are really but few requisites to success. If any are ignorant of the plants or their proper arrangement, read these pages and learn how many simple forms may be adopted to make every house garden alive with plant beauty, and yet require only a half hour per day. A hanging basket or two, a window box or row of bulb glasses, a wardian case or fernery, all are easy. Once set, they need little care. In the other departments of propagation and culture, a little time, patience, and, best of all, trials of experience, will soon render the knowledge easily acquired.

To have some few choice, fragrant, beautiful flowers in mid winter when there is no green thing in sight, save the dense evergreen of the forest, or the garden hedge of spruce, prompts many to an assiduous care, and a hearty devotion to such plant treasures. Yet the recompense is worth the labor.

The matchless beauty which nature once bestowed on the gardens without, is now restored and perpetuated within ; and to many a fair finger deftly handling the tender plant, the exquisite embroidery of the leaf, or coloring of the flower, will form objects for the eye to rest upon with unwearied delight.

WINDOW GARDENING.

Fig. 2.—Design for Window Garden.

CHAPTER II.

CONSTRUCTION, LOCATION AND DESIGNS FOR WINDOW GARDENS.

The Window Gardener has choice of a great number of designs for the gratification of his taste. The Window Box of Evergreens, Ferns, or Ornamental Plants; the Jardiniere, the Hanging Basket, the row of Bulbglasses, the Plant Cabinet, the Fernery, Wardian Case or Conservatory, may all be his : while Flower Stands, Etagere and Mantel Piece Gardens, and other floral elegancies, are of great variety and tasteful constructien. Nothing, however, has so decided an effect as broad leaved plants in the window sill.

Our engraving opposite (Fig. 2) is a sketch of a library window, about 3 feet wide, and 6 high, with book shelves on either side, and a closet below for pamphlets. The window sill is made of extra width, say 14 inches. Here is placed a simple tray of about 3 inches in depth, made to fit the sill exactly: the interior is coated entirely with tin and rendered proof against leakage. The tray is filled with fresh mould from the woods, and then the plants are put in. At each end is an English Ivy, and the spaces between are filled with native hardy ferns, which usually are found out doors near our woods, remaining green down to the coldest winds and frosts of Autumn.

If the front of the box is too plain it may be decorated with a few acorns, and strips of chestnut.

About midway up the window is thrown across a miniature rustic bridge, upon which is still another but narrower tray, with lighter and more delicate ferns, such as the maiden's hair. This rustic bridge may be decorated with a lattice of the bright red dogwood, mingled with the white shoots of the linden. On the top of the window, as a cornice, some rustic branch from one of our wild forest trees, may be selected, twisted and crooked ; yet affording numerous brackets for climbing plants to rest upon. Upon this moss-covered bark the Ivy of the lower box is expected soon to grow up to and crawl over, throwing its tendrils right and left, and filling it full with green foliage. A little hanging basket from the rustic archway, fills out the uniqueness of the picture, and the landscape view beyond is in a measure enhanced by the agreeableness of the standpoint from which we view it.

In some of the finer parts of London, where Window Gardens are dressed in highest elegance, there is a very popular form of Window Garden, consisting of a glass case, projecting beyond the window sashes, somewhat like a little glass bow-windəw. (Fig 3, 4.) These are made in every style, with rustic work in front, or of an architectural character to harmonize with the style of the building

The sills, too, are made broad, and thus afford peculiar conveniences for their safe position. Wealthy citizens who return from the country at close of the summer find these glass gardens ready filled, and charmingly arrayed with ferns, evergreens and flowering plants, which will last throughout the entire winter. In the spring time these give place to Roses, Fuchsias, Pelargoniums, and a variety of other plants suitable for each season. They are exceedingly simple, and besides affording a world of gratification to the inmates of the house they are a great addition to the exterior ornaments of the building. They are not common in this

Fig. 3.

country, and it would be quite an object for some dealer in horticultural elegancies here to make a specialty of them, for as soon as known they will be greatly in demand. The construction is as follows · The lower window sash, is omitted entirely, and the glass case inserted in its place, is of sufficient height to reach to the upper sash. The base should be of one stout slab of slate, resting upon the lower window sill, and extending outward from 1 foot to 2 feet, and the same distance inward. If the window is large, 2 feet each side of the sash will not be too large. An iron frame is then cast of just sufficient length and width to set upon the slab, which may be fastened firmly to it. The glass sides are fitted into the frame beforehand, which is curved at the top, and a tray inside filled with soil holds the plants. In many cases the plant case is double, (*i. e.*,) the lower window sash is not removed at all, but shuts down upon the slab of slate, and the plant case is divided into two parts, each rising and curving upward to the window. Such cases can be made by any manufacturer of glassware and metal casting, but should be well and tightly fitted; as, also, very thick glass should be used as a protection against the weather. For the purposes of examination and cleaning or handling

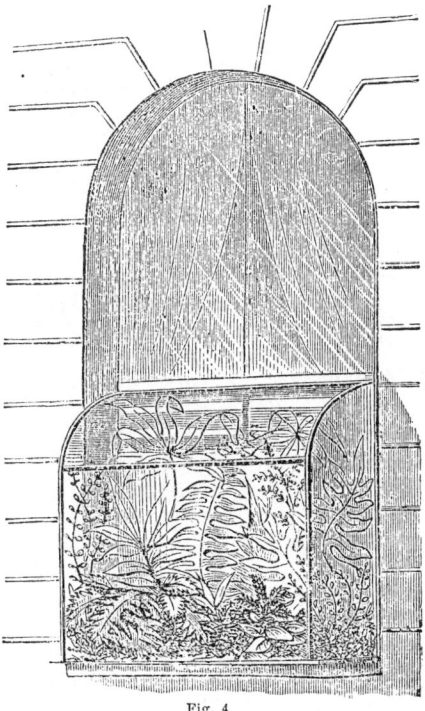

Fig. 4.

the plants, a glass slide or door can be provided in the side within the room. These designs will be found most suitable in our changeable climate for mild weather only, as we fear they would not afford sufficient protection against cold. To some the objection might occur that they hide the view of the street from the interior, but this, with others, might be just the desideratum wished for; yet it will be found in time that it excludes light and air to a considerable degree. Another item must be provided for. Water must necessarily be used for the plants, and there should be a place of escape. The box for holding the soil should be from 4 to 6 inches deep, and the bottom must be covered with broken pieces of charcoal or bricks about the size of walnuts, then a sprinkling of sand and other pieces of brick broken still smaller to about the size of a pea should be mixed with peat, and with this compost the box may be filled up. Cases of this kind are usually found in London, already prepared with plants, only needing the proper dimensions to be soon fitted to any window.

The best plants for these cases are ferns, which require but ordinary attention. and the cultivator will also observe not to place them in a southern window; a

Fig. 5.

northern or western one will be much better for they need little or no heat. As these cases cannot be heated, so no plants should be placed in there which require artificial warmth.

A very pretty design has been originated by a German gardener of a combined window case aquarium and fernery. (Fig. 5.) This occupies the window from the sill to top of the upper sash. The tank within contains slate slabs of considerable height, say one-third of the whole window on the outside of the case, the inner side nearest the room being of glass to afford a view of the interior. This slab is necessary to avoid the effect of the sun's rays which, when passing through a globe or aquarium of water, concentrate upon the floor and burn the carpet Specimens of rock work are introduced at the sides or in the rear of the case; on their top are placed some pots containing ferns drooping over and covering the vacancies all up. If conveniences are at hand a little fountain may be introduced, and be constantly throwing up its tiny streams of water. All this requires great pains of preparation. The window completely shuts out the street view and is lighted only from the top, yet is a great curiosity and with some will be worth the trouble

For planting in such cases as the two just described, the best plants will be the common English Ivy, (*Hedera helix*,) which thrives in confined places of this description and rapidly throws up its green foliage. The *Lygodium scandens* and *Lygodium Japonicum* are lovely climbing ferns, and need copper wires to be trained

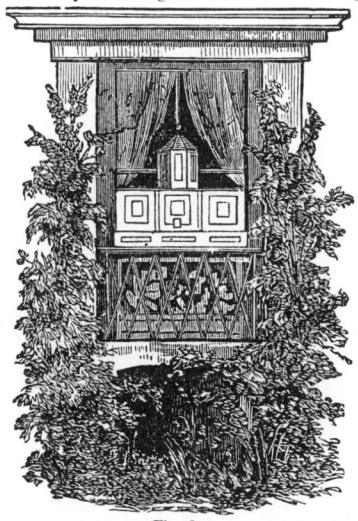

Fig. 6.

to. *Trichomanes radicans, Hymenophyllum Tunbridgense, Asplenium fontanum* are moisture lovers and generally used in furnishing tanks for the aquarium. A suggestion worth heeding is to be remembered: do not commit the error of procuring too large fish for the aquarium; small varieties such as the gold carp are most suitable, and for every two gallon capacity of the water tank, put in one carp. Of water plants the best is *Vallisneria spiralis*, which will grow among pebbles if left undisturbed. *Confervæ* may be introduced and allowed to run over the rock or sides of the aquarium.

A very pretty home design, hardly called a Window Garden, yet affording room for some decoration, is that of a bee hive in the window. Such a hive was actually placed in front of one of the library windows of the late J. C. Loudon, the famous landscape gardener. This window was protected by a verandah, and the front of the hive was placed on a line with its pillars, and was consequently protected from perpendicular rain, but as the excessive heat of summer is equally injurious as rain, he had the hive protected from that and from the sudden influence of either heat or cold, by a casing of broom and heather intertwined. For examining the bees at work, the back of the hive next the window had a sliding door of wood covering a square of plate glass, so that when the door was lifted the bees could be seen at work. The engraving (Fig. 6) also affords to any one an idea of decorating the outside of the window with climbing vines; the *Wistaria* being much the most permanent and rapid growing. This will be found a most inter-

Fig. 7.

esting feature to children and visitors, and it will add much to the convenience of position if the window is low and near the ground.

One of the problems every window gardener has to solve is, to allow his plants all needful light, air and warmth, and yet protect them on the one hand from either the dry heat of the living room warmed by a furnace or stove, and on the other side from penetrating draughts of cold air

This has been solved in many cases already, by the building of plant cabinets, which occupy not only the whole recess of the window, but are built out somewhat into the room, and the entire interior inclosed with glass sides or doors as a partition from the room. In every case that has come to our notice, where plants have been separated alike from the dry injurious air of the living room and the outside atmosphere, there has been the highest success. It is easy to attain a good uniform temperature, and the noxious fumes of the gas from stove, grate or gas burners, are fully protected against. The design introduced here, (Fig. 7,) is a glass case constructed in front of a window and projecting into the room with a door opening into it so that it can be easily entered. It would be well to build the floor of this house of wood, and a little higher than that of the room so that if necessary it can be removed without injury to the house. The lower portions of the case to the height of about two feet should be of wainscot. Inside the

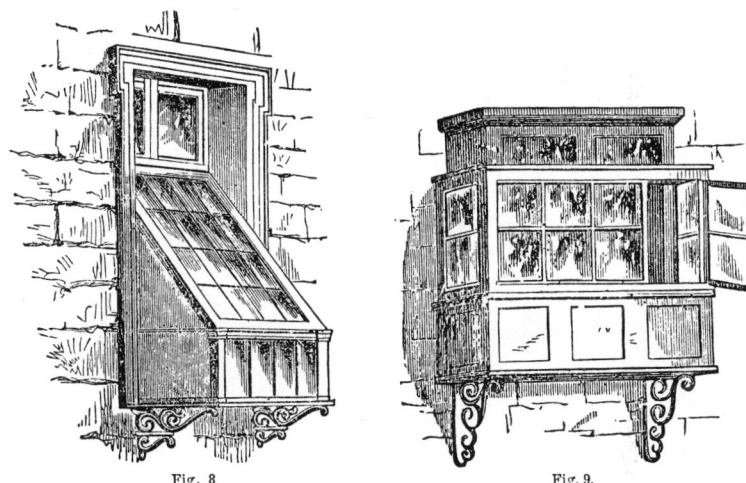

Fig. 8. Fig. 9.

cabinet this paneling is lined with leaden troughs communicating with each other, and having a slight slope towards another trough lower than all the rest; it should be so contrived, that any water draining from the pots or boxes containing the plants, may run off into the lower trough which should have no flower pots in it.

In these troughs should be placed wooden or slate boxes filled with earth in which climbing plants are placed alternately with Orange Trees, Camellias or flowering shrubs, so that they can be seen from the room. It is supposed, also, that the outside window is a bow-window or at any rate projects beyond the sides of the house. It should also have a sliding window at the top or bottom in case ventilation is desired, but cold air must not be admitted without imperative necessity. This design may be on too large a scale for ordinary purposes, but it serves to illustrate the idea that plants always thrive best when placed in rooms entirely by themselves. In such a cabinet a most glorious opportunity is afforded for decorating the sides of the interior with climbing vines, the ivy, convolvulus, or any other with showy colored flowers.

Fig. 10.

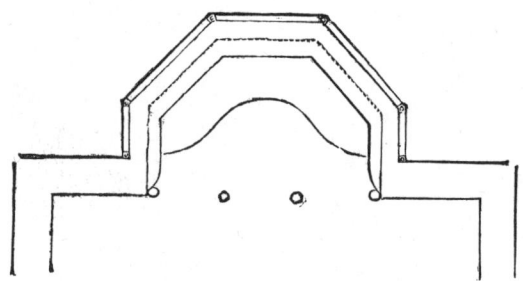

Fig. 11.

Fig. 14 is still another design actually in use in one of our central New York homes. Here is a bow window filled with two boxes supported by legs, each box ten inches deep and filled inside either with earth or separate pots, the interspaces being filled in with moss or earth. The aim is to give a chance to plants with fine contrasts of foliage; Pelargoniums, Petunias, Heliotropes, Fuchsias, Amaranth, Coleus, Begonia, Geraniums, &c. In one end is a Maurandia climbing vine; in the other is a Mexican Cobœa, both twining and drooping over the wires which rise from the centre of the box, and curve towards the sides affording a delicate drapery of green. A hanging basket of moss hangs over each box, the one filled with Oxalis and Tradescantia, the other with Ice Plant. In the vase hanging just over the middle is placed a Kenilworth or Coliseum Ivy. On various brackets below are placed dishes of Ivy, Ferns and Moneywort. A few tall plants may be introduced to advantage, say one large pot full in the centre of each box. In one pot Caladiums, in the other Calla Lilies

Belgian Window Gardens. These are built outside the window altogether. A slab runs out directly from the window sill supported by brackets, and upon this is put a miniature green-house, constructed of glass roof and wooden sides like designs Nos. 8 & 9. These brackets below are generally very ornamental. Two or three shelves are placed inside on a row next to the window well supported and covered with pots. Care is taken not to let the case go too high to obstruct the light from entering the room, and ventilation is secured in Fig. 8, by lifting up slightly the lower portion of the glass roof. The plants are watered and arranged from the rooms within, as the windows do not slide up and down, but open inwardly on hinges.

Fig. 9 is ventilated by a door at the side or in front. An awning may be provided in case of unusual heat from the sun, which will aid in keeping the atmosphere cool, and prolong the flowering considerably during the winter time. A thick covering is needed in cool days, or a vessel of hot water may be placed inside, whose vapor will warm the little room greatly.

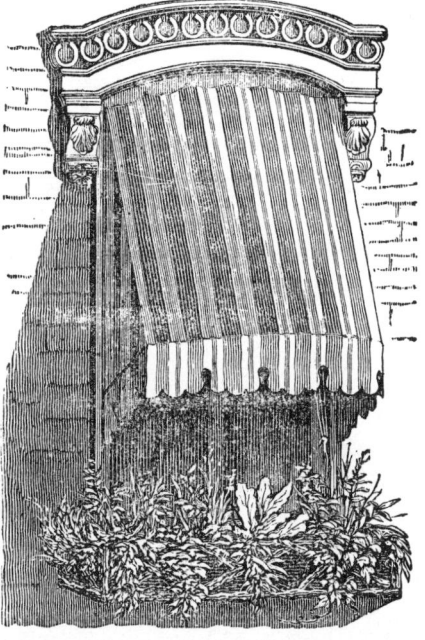

Fig. 12.

Figs. 10 & 11 represent a good continental style of a bow-window, where plants are out of the way of ordinary passing about in the room. Shelves are arranged around the entire window, and upon them are placed the pots of plants. In this case they should be of highly ornamental foliage, and free growth. A curved settee is placed just inside the row, and in front, just at the entrance of the recess, is a table for books.

Fig. 12 is a design for a rustic window box, permanently fastened to the outer side of the window case, decorated with Fuchsias, Ivy, Achyranthus, and drooping vines. An awning with brightly colored stripes adds greatly to the beauty.

Among the more wealthy residents of German cities, a plant cabinet is often found like Fig. 13. This is so made that its back is entirely open, and it can be pushed up close to the window, fitting it snugly. It is elaborately decorated, and quite costly. The door opens into the room, and the tops are ornamented with pots of Cacti and Agaves. This is much the handsomest design for a plant cabi-

Fig. 13.

net ever illustrated. The interior is filled principally with plants of stately growth, Coleus, Calla Lily, Canna, Maranta, Dracæna, Dieffenbachia, &c.

There are other designs of still more simple nature, which may be found in succeeding pages of this book. Window boxes are by far the simplest and most popular, but are adapted mostly to the indoor culture of bulbs We have noticed frequently the late introduction of tile boxes, filling the entire width of the window, and placed just inside the panes of glass, filled with nothing but young plants of the Arbor Vitae. Their delicate, feathery green foliage contrasts well with the white curtains just behind, and the whole form one of the easiest, yet most unique styles of window gardening.

The Location of the Window Garden

A good location or exposure is desirable. There are plants which love the shade. Pansies, Sweet Violets, and some of the variegated plants, will grow and bloom if not placed directly in the sun's ray ; but Roses, Geraniums, Heliotropes, Verbenas, Daphnes, Azaleas, &c., must be near the glass, and under the direct influence of the light, if we would have them flourish. An exposure where the sun can strike unobstructed from its first appearance above the horizon in the morning, until one or two o'clock, P. M., is much the most desirable. A southern or southeastern window is the best, next is an eastern exposure, then a western one, and the north worst of all. At a northern one, little but Pansies and Sweet Violets will grow, though Camellias delight in a cool, moist atmosphere, and will often flourish at such a window with but little sunshine. The plants must have all the sunshine you can bestow upon them, but at night they should be kept in the dark; and as all plants in summer are cooler at night than in the day time, those that are grown in windows should also be cooler. This point is perhaps not as well understood as it should be, for there are persons so fearful

Fig. 14.—A Sitting Room Window.

that their plants will become chilled, that they turn all the heat of their furnaces upon them at night, and the gas-light joined with it, increases the irritation; so that the plants are kept in an unnatural state when they ought to be at rest, for plants need sleep and do sleep; so the effect of unreasonable light and heat is very exhausting. Drop the curtains over the plants to exclude them from the light of the room, or pin newspapers around them during the evening. Nothing is so handy and useful in protecting them from frost as newspapers. They will frequently preserve a plant when the mercury falls nearly to freezing point. Neither should plants be chilled. Avoid the extreme of rendering them too cool, but maintain a good medium temperature. Rooms whose thermometer reaches 80 to 85° during the day, and then falls to 30 or 35° at night, will never keep plants in good health.

Size of Windows.

The larger the better if you want to grow many plants. Bow windows are always liked, and generally considered the best, as they afford exposure to the sun at all hours of the day, if they face the south. The larger the panes, also the better. The best style of window, not bow, is to have a good sill, say not less than six inches wide on each side of the sash; if eight or ten inches, so much the better; this affords room for a fine sill or rustic window box, which may be changed at intervals from the inner sill to the outer one jutting beyond the edge of the sash. Boxes for this style of window should be six inches deep. Sometimes double boxes may be desired, one on each side of the window, in which case the outer box should contain low growing evergreens, and the interior one bulbs. It is usual, also, to cover the sills with paper before setting the boxes down. Still this is not necessary where there is no danger from leaking. If the window is low, and near the ground, climbing vines may be trained upward over the window; this is more fully described under head of balcony gardening.

Our windows differ so much in size that every one must shape their preparations entirely according to their conveniences; but if a sill, either permanent or temporary, can be constructed on the outside of the window, it will be found of convenient and constant use

CHAPTER III.

General Management of Window Gardens.

In-door plants naturally require more care than those grown in the open air, for nature supplies all the needs of the latter; but the secrets of successful growth and profuse blooming in the house are enumerated in the following few essential rules of management:

1st. Give them plenty of light during the day, and darkness with a cooler temperature at night.

2d. A good supply of fresh air, when the sun shines brightest and warmest; in mild days the upper sashes may be lowered a little, and the cool air will blow over the plants instead of directly upon them.

3d. Perfect cleanliness, which is very important, for if the plants are covered with dust, they cannot grow, and will frequently die; their leaves are their lungs; frequent syringing will keep the leaves moist and clean.

4th. A proper amount of moisture; a dry atmosphere is fatal

5th. A good compost or soil, in which their roots can luxuriate and send forth vigorous branches, leaves and flowers.

6th. Get good healthy plants to start out with; plants that have been blooming all through the summer, or for several months previous will not do well, new ones are best, or plants that were used the previous winter, and have rested during the summer, will also answer, but in general it is best to get new plants

7th. Keep only a few plants; too many in the window will make close crowding; pots should never be set two or three deep on top of each other.

8th. A uniform temperature of 60° to 70° in the day time and 40° to 45° in the night, should be steadily mantained.

9th. Different places should be provided for different plants. A sunny window with a temperature of 45° to 50,° will suit roses, geraniums, &c., best; Begonias, Coleus, Cissus discolor, want a still warmer place of 60° to 70°, and yet but little or no sun light directly upon them. On the other hand, Heliotropes, and Bouvardias want all the sun possible, with a temperature in the daytime of 60° to 75°.

Sunlight.

Plenty of sunlight is the gardener's first requisite. If the location for this purpose is not right, the plants will not be healthy. If the plants are well placed in a good light, then the pots must be turned occasionally so that all sides may receive it equally. It will be well also to put flower stands or racks of pots on wheels, so that the whole may be changed at once, or wheeled away, if the room needs cleaning. Care must be taken to avoid rapid transition from darkness to the light, for sudden and violent changes are as trying to plant life as human life Too much warmth will destroy tender leaves nearly as soon as too much cold. Then again, plants should be placed as near the light as possible; in rooms far away from the glass window, the plants will be weak, pale and of spindling growth. If they could receive light directly from overhead, they would be better than from the side. The ordinary variations of day and night have their corresponding effects on plants, since it is said that they inhale under the influences of light, and respire in the dark. The glass of the window should also be rubbed or washed clean. The most gaily colored flowers will be produced at a south window, but a north window has its advantage, in that it may be used for plants already in bloom, and will keep them much longer in perfection. For north windows, Camelias, Cytisuses, Primulas and Alpine Auriculas, will find the cool moisture they need, and will bloom in great beauty if properly attended to and kept from frost. Bulbs, if placed in the sunlight, will have their brilliancy of color greatly enhanced, yet if not changed occasionally in position, their flower stems will bend over and have an unsightly appearance.

Temperature.

The greatest success will be found to come from a uniform temperature of 45 or 50° at night, and 60 to 75° in the day time; 80° is too hot except for only some plants of semi-tropical character. Under no circumstances should the temperature go below 35°. If your living rooms, where your plants are placed must be considerably warmer than this in the former part of the night, then set the plants on the floor, shade from the light until the time of retiring, and then return them to the window sill or flower stand. Perhaps from no other cause than this, too great heat, during the day and long continued at night, our city grown plants grow so sickly and lanky in appearance. Once or twice a week will be sufficient for turning pots around. If this little item is not attended to, you cannot grow finely formed plants, and more than half their beauty depends upon their shape. If a closet or small room opening out of the sitting room can be devoted to plants and yet be well lighted, they will flourish far better than in the common room, for they can have a cooler atmosphere and less dust.

The same object could however be accomplished in a far more tasteful manner by enclosing the window recess with another glass window or partition. The outside glass protects the plants from the cold, the inside ones from undue heat and gas, while between the two there is a happy mean in which plant culture cannot fail to be successful. If however this is not done, and the window panes are made of double glass there will be little danger of their freezing on a cold night. It would be well to have one pane fitted with a hinge, which can be opened to air the plants. But to avoid this a heavy curtain can be placed at the window, and pulled down at night, to protect from cold air, while newspapers may be pinned around the plants to protect them from the bright light of the evening. The amateur must also study the characteristics of his plants, for one temperature will not answer for all. The Rose needs a cool atmosphere, yet moderately moist. The Fuschia is fond of both warmth and moisture, but needs occasional shading when the sun is too hot. The Coleus prefers plenty of heat and moisture, and would be satisfied never to have the thermometer go below 70° by night or day. The Geranium seems to accommodate itself to all circumstances, being the most easily grown of all window plants, and apparently needs only plenty of light and air, and average warmth.

Plants at night.

Plants need rest. Uniform darkness at night with lower temperature, is one of the conditions of treatment, but sometimes there may be a sudden change of temperature in the outer air, and in consequence thereof some one or more plants of the window garden may be frozen. Do not throw them away, but cut the branches back as far as frozen, or near to the soil, then water slightly and do not let the plant get quite as warm as before; if it has any life it will soon show buds and branches. Plants should be treated very much like human beings; a frosted finger should be warmed gradually, so should a frozen plant. Some plants if frosted, like Fuschias, will sprout from the roots and make a strong growth; others will send out strong, healthy flowering branches from the stem near the roots. A very simple plan to restore frosted plants is to transfer them at once to a dark cellar and shower them plentifully with water; keep them here two or three weeks and they will gradually recover their health again.

Another point is often discussed, whether *plants are injurious in rooms at night*. We think it unwise to have too many in a room; a few here and there are of little influence. Strong scented plants are injurious to have in the room at night. The Tuberose, Hyacinth and Jessamine, &c., are too sweet to be allowed to remain in a bedroom at night, and should not be patronized for this purpose by invalids. The sensations of the individual are often a good guide. After sleeping in a room with plants, the morning finds the sleeper inactive, feeling as if his night's rest had been heavy, the air of the room also does not seem pure, and the perfume peculiar. All the indications are sufficient to show the air is vitiated, and fresh air is needed as much by the individual as the plant.

Fresh Air.

Ventilation is absolutely necessary; therefore give it. Whenever the weather is mild open the window. *Too little fresh air* and too much warmth are formidable obstacles to success in house gardening. Plants that are kept shut up in warm rooms become very sensitive and are far more liable to suffer from a sudden fall in the temperature; but if they are frequently exposed to the fresh air they are better able to bear these changes of climate which often occur so unexpectedly. Those who live in close heated rooms can never make their flowers bloom in winter with any vigor. Some think that any atmosphere not inconvenient to men and women is good enough for the plant. It will live just as the human being lives, but it does so in sufferance rather, for it will not grow and bloom in perfect beauty. A very few handsome flowering vines are much to be preferred to spindling plants, pictures of misery, like their owners, overheated and crowded into close unhealthy unventilated quarters. In our fever to provide sufficient warmth in our rooms against the cold, we stop up every crack in our windows, every crevice of our doors; then with furnaces, grates or stoves at almost fever heat we get warmth enough to bid defiance to the chilling atmosphere. Rarely are we satisfied with a temperature in the room of less than 75°, and this must be constantly maintained from early morning till late at night. A draught of fresh air would quicken your blood and put a little more spirit into your countenances; still you aim to avoid it. Yet for the sake of your plants do it at least once a day. Throw open the doors and air the room thoroughly. This can be done at time for meals when it is usually vacant. The windows should not be opened directly upon the plants. Some other window or door away from the plants may be opened. It should be done also at the middle of the day when the outer air is mildest.

Cleanliness.

Here close attention is again required. Plants require regular care. They cannot be watered and cared for once a week and the rest of the time left to themselves, but they demand a daily amount of time to be spent upon them. Every morning when house cleaning is in order, the plants must be watered and cleaned. You will see how necessary this is, if you look at the nature of the plants, how they live. Like our skins, the leaves of plants are perforated with hundreds of minute pores through which they breathe, exhaling oxygen and inhaling carbon, and also giving out and inhaling moisture. If these pores are filled up with dust the plant cannot perform these functions and its life either ceases or stands still; it is not possible for it to grow or bloom. The dust of our living rooms is very injurious to the health of every plant. Unless it is removed, you may as well give up all hope of making your window favorites succeed. Frequent washing and watering are absolutely essential. For close handling of leaves, a soft sponge is of great service, for it can be used in the parlor without danger of dripping from the watering-pot. Wash each leaf separately and see that both sides of it are clean. To shower a plant turn it sideways over a tub of water or a sink; sprinkle it thoroughly with the watering-pot. If the plants are too large to handle in this manner set the pots or tubs into a larger one and either sprinkle or syringe every branch and leaf. You must improvise summer showers if you would induce summer growth. It is not enough to water the earth in the pot. The whole plant requires it. Frequent waterings are the most beneficial culture that you can bestow upon your plants. To be sure they are not easily given and will entail upon you some work.

When sweeping and dusting your rooms, throw newspapers or a light cloth over them; this will prevent the dust from settling upon the leaves, and help materially toward keeping them clean.

Whenever a warm rain falls, and the temperature stands at 50° or 55,° set all the plants out of doors, and they will be greatly refreshed and strengthened. It does not follow, however, that the whole plant is watered by being thus placed out doors; the leaves of the plant may be broad and shield the pot and roots; so do not forget to give these a chance also. If the leaves of plants are very dirty, warm water with a little soap and the use of the sponge or syringe, will remove all dirt. Exposure to the fresh air is not as dangerous as many would suppose, provided the temperature is mild. They are, in fact, benefited by such exposure and become far more hardy and able to resist sudden changes of temperature, much better than if kept constantly confined to the room.

Very few have any idea of how fast the dust accumulates in a room; it is in fact one of the greatest enemies the housewife has to contend with. A short time only, suffices to see the leaves of a plant covered with dust; if it is not removed, they soon get brown and wither; and it is really delightful, after giving them a good washing, to see how bright and shining are the leaves and how greatly they have been invigorated.

Watering Plants.

When shall I water my plants? is a vexed question, asked perhaps more frequently than any other by the beginner. This depends entirely upon the nature of the plant, for some need more water than others, and yet a soil thoroughly wet is totally unfit for plant-growing. The real idea each cultivator should aim for is to supply the plants with water, which may drain rapidly through the pots, yet sufficient be retained to give a good moist soil for the plant to live in. If the water passes away rapidly it will need replacing frequently. It is generally a sign of health when the soil is well drained and the plant uses up the supply of water quickly.

Watering should be supplied with a careful hand, for many parlor gardeners have an unrestrainable belief in the hydropathic process. To them there is only one orthodox rule: if the plants will wither up or are troubled with insects and do not grow as healthy and freely as they might, they drench it with a flood of cold water; so it is a fact, that more plants perish in the hands of the inexperienced, from having too copious a supply than too little. There are others again more cautious in their applications of water, who are, on the other hand, totally heedless of drainage, and let the water stand in the saucers under the pots, or in boxes without drainage, causing mould and sogginess of soil, rendering the roots weak and unhealthy.

The purposes of watering should be better understood. 1st. Water supplies to the roots fertilizing matter, contained in itself, and 2d. It converts the nourishment of the soil into a liquid form more readily fit for absorption by the roots. The roots can obtain it only when the soil is dampened.

Never give water when the soil is moist to the touch, but wait until it is dry.

Few plants thrive if water is around them constantly; yet Lobelias, Callas, Ivies, etc., are very thirsty and like to drink at their own will. Indeed they will not bloom or grow well unless you allow them so to do.

The healthiest plants require water the most frequently; and yet it may appear a contradiction to say that the plants which contain the most watery tissues, grow in the dryest places. The Cacti often supply moisture to the wild cattle of the plains of Mexico; the animals break through their thorny exteriors with their hoofs, and then eat the moist morsels contained within, which quench their thirst

Water, cold from the well or pump, is not suitable for plants, unless of a temperature of 60°. Rain water is best, for this is supposed to contain some little ammonia from the sky.

The best rule in all cases is to use water warm to the hands. Some florists advise water no colder than the atmosphere. We believe it generally best to use it *warmer*. In cool mornings it should be lukewarm, say not under 55°. Some cultivators say they have used hot water for sickly plants heated to a temperature from 200° to 250°, and have believed this to be the cause of their subsequent luxuriant growth and production of flowers of the greatest beauty; but trials like this are not to be encouraged, and warm water of 75° to 150°, will do just as well and have far less danger from scalding. Over 150° is neither necessary nor safe. A lady is said to have once watered her plants with the tea that remained in her pot after the breakfast was finished. Her plants grew in wonderful beauty and luxuriance, and she attributes it to the magic effects of the tea; yet she has forgotten it was better due to the warmth of the water than any fancied virtue. Some plants demand more water than others. Fuchsias, for instance, while in bloom often require water both morning and evening, and nearly all plants desire more when in flower than at any other time. The supply of water must be regulated according to the demand of the plants. Calla Lilies will absorb water two or three times as quickly as any other plant of the Window Garden. If rainwater cannot be easily obtained and hard water is the only source at hand, add a little soda to it and let it stand for a while; use a small piece, say a small nugget of the size of a pea, to every gallon; on that pour about a pint of boiling water and then fill it up with cold water. It will be quite warm, and a thorough drenching overhead and in the pots will vastly improve their color and health. A drop or two of hartshorn will also correct hard water somewhat. In watering, never wet merely the surface, but moisten the whole ball of earth in the pot. If the ball should yet be very dry set the whole pot in a pail of warm water till it is soaked through. The morning is the best time of the day for watering. A common hand-brush made of broomcorn dipped into warm water and shaken over the plants will imitate a summer shower, but its tiny drops may spatter against the window glass. A toy watering-pot, such as is used for children, is very useful for Window Gardening. If oil cloth is laid under the stand it can be used without much if any injury to the carpet or furniture. Care should be taken that the pots have good drainage, for then all surplus water will run into the

Fig. 15.

saucer, which may be emptied as fast as filled. In warm mild weather when plants absorb a great deal of moisture it will do no harm to leave a little in the saucer. Among other details to be observed in watering, the following items of caution are to be observed: Some plants should never be wetted on the leaves. Take the Begonia Rex, whose foliage, so large and grand, has an exquisite coloring; if its leaves were to be sponged with cold water, and the plant left out on the balcony or open air, it would probably die very soon; but a Camelia can be treated the same way and not be injured in the slightest. The reasons for it are good. The last plant has a hard shiny leaf, which can resist rough treatment; but the other has a succulent tender leaf easily affected. The novice then may generally find it true that plants with soft porous and hairy leaves should be very cautiously wetted overhead, but plants with hard varnished leaves may be watered frequently. Tepid water should be invariably used even down to the height of summer. If plants get infested with vermin, a sponging with soap and water made into a lather, will clear them. Then follow with clear water to remove the soap. It is also a good rule to observe that the colder the weather the less water must be given; and when plants are at rest, done growing, they need very little indeed

Plants in cases may be watered once a week, for evaporation there is confined, but in open rooms once a day is sufficient. Some plants, who delight in very moist situations, need it twice a day. Never water when the sun is hot.

If the soil of the pot gets too hard, loosen it a little with a fork, or plunge it into a tub of water. Take pains to have good drainage, and beyond this little trouble will be experienced.

The Philosophy of Watering

is worth studying. Plants are constantly throwing off or evaporating moisture from their leaves, and at the same time the roots must be taking up an equal supply. If then on examining the soil in a flower-pot, you discover that it is moist for an unusually long time, you may be sure that something is wrong, either the roots do not take it up readily, or drainage is imperfect. Healthy plant action needs air as well as moisture. A soggy soil excludes air, and, as a result, our plants soon show drooping leaves and unhealthy branches. Drainage is to plants what digestion is to the human system, keeping everything in perfect action. Water and air enjoy a healthy circulation unimpeded, and plants which are growing freely and vigorously, with strong roots, will take up the moisture of the pots regularly. Mr. Meehan, who has studied plant physiology more thoroughly than any other American, sums up this subject in the following concise paragraph:

"A wet soil is totally unfit for plant growing. A plant standing 24 hours in water is irreparably injured. A Hyacinth, to be sure, will live one season in water; but all the matter of the flower which goes to water is prepared the year before, and after flowering, the bulb is exhausted and almost worthless.

"A good soil for plant growing, therefore, is not one which will hold water, but one in which water will pass away.

"The soil itself is composed of minute particles, through which air spaces abound. The water must be just enough to keep these particles moist, and the air in the spaces is thus kept in the condition of moist air. The roots traverse these air spaces, and it is, therefore, *moist air* which roots want, and not water.

"If it were water simply which plants wanted, we should cork up the bottom of the hole in the flower pot, and prevent the water getting away. Instead of this, we try to hasten the passing of the water through as much as possible, by not only keeping the hole clear, but often by putting broken pieces in the bottom to hasten the drainage. A plant will generally be the healthiest, therefore, which wants water the oftenest. If it does not want water, it is in a bad way. And more water will make the matter worse.

"How often to water them, will be according to how easy the water passes away. If, when you pour water on earth it disappears almost instantly, it would be safe to water such plants every day.

"The constant aim of the cultivator should be to keep the soil of such a consistence that a moist atmosphere shall always be present in the air spaces existing through it.

Moisture of the Atmosphere.

The atmosphere of our houses, as we have intimated before, is not only too dry for successful plant culture, but it breeds insects of various kinds which will injure their growth.

We have noticed that plants kept in kitchen windows where the air is charged with moist vapors from the boiling of water over the stove or range, and where the outside doors are frequently opened, and fresh air supplied, will often develop into surprising luxuriance and beauty. We can call to mind even now a farm kitchen in the coldest portion of our most northern states, where Roses, Carnations and Verbenas, grow finely, and are covered with a summery profusion of buds and flowers. These are usually the most difficult plants to bring into bloom in parlor windows, because they are apt to be so infested with minute red spiders, and the green aphis, scale or mealy bug.

It is the moisture in the air which tends to restrain and drive away such disagreeable intruders. The heated air of the house can be kept moist by placing an evaporating pan upon or in our furnaces, and over our stoves we can place a large fire-proof dish that must be daily filled with water.

If the surfaces of the soil in pots is covered with moss, it retards the evaporation of water; this practice is generally advisable only for those plants which require much water, such as Calla Lilies, Fuchsias, Camellias, &c. Pots that are imbedded in moss are always kept moist, and if a table is constructed just the height of the window, with a rim fastened around each side three inches in depth, and the whole lined with zinc, the pots can be set in it, and the moss stuffed in on all sides. When watering is needed, set it back from the window and sprinkle with a fine watering pot.

The Soil.

The most easily available material for a compost by the ordinary gardener, will

WINDOW GARDENING. 31

be rich loam, sand, and thoroughly decayed cow manure. This should be mixed in the proportion of one half of the loam to one quarter each of the sand and manure. Leaf mould is also another grand material which every plant loves to grow in, and it will pay to secure a good quantity of it. The older and more decomposed the manure and leaf mould, the better they are, and every plant grower should keep a well prepared compost heap for his plants. A good compost, when all the material is handy, is composed of one fourth of the above elements of leaf mould, sand, loam and manure. To those who live in cities and can not get this conveniently, it is best either to buy your plants already potted, or go to a good florist and buy a good quantity of right compost; he can usually supply it at cheaper rate than it can be purchased anywhere else.

Keep this heap well filled, and no one must fail to bear in mind that the soil of every one of his pots needs changing and replenishing, or else it becomes exhausted, and the plants dwindle and languish for needed food.

Garden loam is often used by those in the country and found to answer, but if it should contain any clay, a little sand must be added. The sand itself is of no fertilizing effect, but is valuable in assisting the aeration of the soil and helping the drainage. Well rotten turf is another handy and valuable material, containing considerable quantity of vegetable mould. If used, put the coarser pieces at the bottom along with some pebbles or broken pieces of crockery, then fill in the finer mould to about half an inch from the surface. The soil must not be allowed to cake up, but be occasionally stirred up deep, so that air may have access to the roots

Leaf mould is more highly prized by gardeners than anything else that can be procured. Every autumn the leaves are gathered in heaps, wheeled by the barrow load to a good location, and there left exposed to the rain and the action of the weather for sometimes two or three years. Here it decomposes and becomes rotten. Then it is mixed with good turf mould, also left to rot for a year or two, and finally chopped up; then add the sand, decomposed manure and some peat well minced to small pieces. This is considered the very best material for pots, or borders in green-houses or conservatories. A good pile of it is always maintained. It is rather an advantage than otherwise to have a few lumps in each pot; they prevent the soil from becoming too solid.

A compost for *Camellias, Roses, Geraniums, &c.*, should be one part river sand, one part leaf mould, two parts turf or garden mould. For *Cacti*, use two parts coarse sand, three parts leaf and turf mould, one part peat, and a little broken plaster.

For *Azaleas, Ericas*, and most *New Holland plants*, take four parts peat two parts sand, one part garden or turf mould, one part leaf mould.

Soil for bulbous roots should be light; place them in the centre of the pots about half imbedded in the light earth, then cover them with leaf or fine turf mould.

For drainage purposes, put in the bottom of each pot either a layer of powdered charcoal, or small broken pieces of brick or old mortar to the depth of a least an inch ; over this there may be a slight sprinkling of sand ; still it may be omitted if it has previously been well incorporated in the compost. In general it should never be less than one fifth the whole material of the compost, and one fourth will be best in most cases

Forest mould scraped up under the branches of pine or other forest trees, or the soil taken from under the sods of droppings in cow pastures, will be found useful in imparting a vigorous growth to plants

Amateurs sometimes choose earth from the back yards of their city residences ; this is rarely ever suitable, and often its effects can be seen in the half dead and weak look of the plants, who seem to be languishing for nourishment. This soil is rarely ever fertilized, and usually is either the filling in from the street or cellar It may be fit to grow grass upon, but not to put in the pots of house plants.

There are some plants which require an imperative admixture of peat and loam, such as Ericas, Azaleas and Daphne. There is no substance which can be substituted for it, and produce success. Earth for pots should rarely ever be sifted, put it in just as it is; lumpy and crude, so much the better

In potting your plants and planting them out, be very careful to press the earth very tightly and closely around the roots and stalks of the plants ; half the secret of successful pot culture lies in *potting plants.*

Hard wooded plants should be potted rather firmly, and soft wooded ones should be left rather free and loose.

In repotting plants, take the plant that is to be repotted, turn it upside down, with your left hand across the mouth of the pot, and the stem of the plant between the fingers, give the pot a few raps on a pan on the table, lift up the pot and you have the plant and the ball of earth in your hand.

Examine it carefully, and if any worms appear, pick them out, or if the earth is full of healthy roots, and they are matted around the sides of it, the plant requires a pot one size larger than that in which it has grown.

Place the ball of earth and the plant directly in the centre of the new pot, and fill it up all around with fresh soil, pressing it firmly down either with the fingers or a flat stick; cover the "ball" with fresh earth half an inch in depth ; strike the bottom of the pot several times against a flat substance, and again press the soil tightly around the roots. Loose planting is a fruitful source of the non-success attending the gardening of amateur florists. Place your plants in the shade for two or three days to allow their roots to become accustomed to the charge of quarters. A healthy, abundantly rooted plant, requires a pot one size larger, but, if the plant you turn out should not show its roots on the outside, it needs no change of quarters, still it may need fresh soil, and if the earth seems poor and gritty it is best to give it..

If in examination of your pots you should find some plant injured by injudicious waterings, its roots rotten, and soil soddened, then cut or tear away the decayed parts, turn out the wet soil, take a pot of the smaller size, and

WINDOW GARDENING. 33

with a lighter soil give it another chance for life, watering it sparingly until the foliage shows its return to health and strength.

Never pot a plant that has its ball of earth quite dry, for you cannot give it water afterward. All the water you pour upon it will run down the fresh soil at the sides of the pot, leaving the plant to perish with drought. Sometimes in potting plants, you will find a large brown root coiled up in the pot like a snake. Cut it off close to the main root and put this plant in a pot of smaller size, and very soon fresh and more nourishing roots will take its place. Such roots are often found in pots of Geraniums. This piece of root can be made to grow by cutting it into 3 inch lengths, and planting them in pots of sandy loam, leaving a quarter of an inch of the root uncovered, and keeping them warm and moist.

In placing plants in pots in the open air, either sink them in the borders or on the grass. Be sure to scatter coal or wood ashes underneath them, to prevent worms from entering the pots and the soil from becoming clogged.

Fertilizers for Stimulating House Plants.

All plants will grow much finer if stimulants are given, say at least once a week. A very fine liquid fertilizer can be made out of horse and cow manure. Take an old bucket for the purpose, put into it several shovels full of manure, to which add one pint of charcoal dust, this neutralizes its odor, add to it plenty of boiling water, let it cool, and apply to the plant. It should not be given too strong, but about the color of weak tea. The bucket can stay filled up with water for six weeks or two months as it is needed, then throw away its contents and begin again.

Guano water, a decoction of Peruvian guano, makes a good stimulant. It should be applied once a week to the roots, taking care not to touch the leaves with it. To one gallon of hot water, add one large tablespoonful of guano; stir until it is dissolved. Hen manure may be substituted and used in about the same quantity.

When used carefully, either are excellent, and give the plants a bright, vigorous green.

Ammonia water stimulates growth very satisfactorily. Dissolve ¼ ounce of pulverized ammonia in a gallon of water, and it will prove more grateful to the plants even than rain water which also contains ammonia. A teaspoonful of *aqua ammonia* added to a gallon of warm water will be of same efficacy. *Flour of bone,* when it can be obtained in the form of powder, easily soluble in water, is still more suitable, for it contains other elements of plant nutrition. Used in moderate quantities, not over a tablespoonful to a gallon of warm water, it will give the plants a healthy impetus; give a sufficient quantity to wet the whole ball of earth and pour off the surplus water that runs into the saucer. A special fertilizer used to advantage by some, is composed as follows: take of sulphate of ammonia four ounces, nitrate of potash two ounces, white sugar one ounce, add one pint of hot water; when dissolved, cork tightly and add a teaspoonful to every gallon of water used for watering; six or eight drops of this liquid can be poured into the water of a hyacinth glass, and the flowers will be much finer

All these special stimulants must be used with caution, be well diluted, applied not oftener than once a week and once in three weeks will be sufficient for the hyacinth.

Pinching

Plants should be kept in good shape by pinching off their shoots from time to time, so as to avoid an outward spindling appearance, straggling branches can never be handsome; but if their shoots are nipped or pinched in every month or so, they will grow bushy and have many more blossoms and leaves. Fig 16

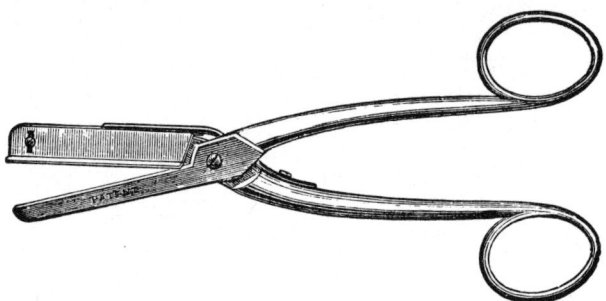

Fig. 16.

shows a good pruning scissors Fuchsias and Pelargoniums are generally stopped once or twice before they flower. When the shoots have grown about three leaves their ends are pinched out; this gives three or four shoots instead of one, and increases the proportion of blossoms, but keeps the plant dwarf The *training* of plants is also a matter of taste, usually the form of a half circle is most preferred. Fuchsias trained to single stakes and allowed to droop down are natural objects of beauty Every gardener has his fancy. Nothing is so pleasing as to see a rose trained to stakes in pots bent completely back to the pot, in the shape of a semi-circle—every branch covered with buds just ready to bloom.

General Suggestions.

1. All plants have a season of rest; therefore discover what season is peculiar to each, and transplant at that time. 2. The best time for taking cuttings is when the plants are in their most active state of growth, and this is before flowering. 3. Profuse bloomings exhaust the strength of plants, therefore cut off all flower buds as soon as their petals fall, and do not let the seed pods mature unless you desire to raise seeds. 4. All bulbs and tubers should be planted before they begin to shoot; if suffered to form leaves and roots in the air, they waste their strength. 5. Never remove the leaves from bulbs after flowering until they are quite dead. As long as the leaves retain life they are employed in preparing nourishment and transmitting it to the roots. 6. Window

plants are more liable to be injured by frost than plants in the ground, because the fibres of the roots cling to the sides of the pots and are more quickly affected by the chilling air. 7. The faster a plant grows, the farther apart are the leaves, the more distant the side branches, and the more bare appears the stem. Richness of foliage can never be attained when leaves become thus scattered. By keeping a lower temperature, especially at night, there will be a slower and more desirable growth, and conducive to compactness of habit in plants. 8. No plants can bear sudden contrasts of temperature without injury, therefore bring nothing directly from a heated room to the cool open air 9. By checking the growth of leaves and branches you throw more strength into the flowers; this is why the terminal shoots of many plants should be pinched off to increase their vigor. 10 Avoid excessive heat. Plants often languish in a hot temperature while their owners cannot imagine why they do not grow, forgetting that the atmosphere is already too warm for even human beings. Suggestions like these will show that although Window Gardens require some skill and experience in good management, yet there is nothing abstruse or difficult to prevent any one from undertaking the care of one which needs only a reasonable degree of thought and attention to make it a constant delight.

CHAPTER IV.

Special Care of Window Gardens.

In Winter

The beauties of the flower garden are gone, and we are now left to solace ourselves with any green thing we can coax by artificial help to grow and bloom during the long winter months, till spring returns again. Naturally enough we hate to lose the sight of the flowers, and graceful flutter of the green leaves, so we strive to prolong our joy, as far as possible, under many difficulties through unsuitable seasons.

During the winter seasons the chief requisites of success, are plenty of sunshine, an atmosphere not too dry or close, a mild uniform temperature, and especial attention to cleanliness, watering and daily care.

Plants which receive only a few moments of attention a day and then forgotten, soon become a disgrace, and the window garden becomes a nuisance.

In the open ground plants will flourish if left to themselves, but when grown in a pot, they are under artificial restraints and conditions, and must become an object of constant attention. This very necessity of the case renders window gardening of so much greater interest than out door gardening.

Plants at night should be in the dark, as that is their natural condition so that they may rest, and yet it is equally important that they should be freely exposed to the sun as long as light lasts.

So, especially in the winter months, when there is comparatively so little sunlight, place them as closely to the windows as they can be well managed, if not, they will become unsightly, drawn and weak. The more light that a plant receives the more freely can it absorb carbon and breathe out oxygen; so if you wish your plants to be purifiers of the air, be sure that they have plenty of light, and keep both blinds and curtains from obstructing it.

The necessity for air in *the winter* is no less imperative than the demand for light. In order to cultivate Geraniums successfully, a constant supply of fresh air is very needful. Roses, Verbenas, and indeed all plants demand it.

When plants are first brought into the house they should not be stimulated, but allowed a little time to become accustomed to their new quarters; and they will often wither a little from the want of fresh air, so let the windows be open all day, if it is sunny, and accustom them by degrees to the change of 'temperature.

It is not desirable to allow them to remain out too late in the season, but they should be housed before any danger of frost arises; a slight chill will frequently injure them greatly, especially the Coleus, and all sub tropical plants unused to our cold autumn winds.

They can be placed on a protected piazza, and covered at night with some mats or sheets, but the true lover of house plants does not feel at ease until all her pets are standing in their winter quarters; then the cold chilly winds may blow, and Jack Frost's icy fingers pinch with blackening touches all that they can reach; the household flowers are safe beyond his dreaded touch.

Do not crowd your plant stands or windows, give to each plant room to stretch forth its branches and leaves, if you would have it bloom in vigor and beauty; untidy straggling plants are always detestable.

Every dead leaf must be removed and every fading flower, and the leaf must not remain in the pots, but be taken away; cleanliness is so important that no damp leaves or decaying flowers should be left. Window plants suffer chiefly in the winter months from indiscriminate waterings, allowing them to go dry for two or three days and then soaking them for a week.

Many a lady cannot imagine why her plants do not grow and bloom as luxuriantly as at her opposite neighbor's. But it is the lack of daily atttention that makes the difference. One lady buys her plants because it is the fashion to have them in the windows; the other loves her plants as a part of herself, sees in them an individuality; a glimpse perhaps of something beautiful beyond this world's plain realities, and it is not a care for her to attend to their necessities, but rather a privilege.

In the winter time the familiar question is asked over and over again: "How am I to know when my plants need watering?" Watch them carefully, and they will tell you; wilted leaves, drooping branches, and yellow shades show that they are water-clogged; they must be allowed a respite.

Turn up the soil as heretofore directed, with a stout hair pin, and if it is dry give more water; if not, abstain from it.

Success in window gardening depends greatly in never permitting the plants to suffer from any neglect.

When you water, give it copiously, and if the next day the plants have enough pass them by; but there are always some in a window or a stand of plants that desire it, so carry round the watering pot every day, take the time either before or after breakfast, have a special hour, and never forget it. There is more danger of giving too much water during the winter, than in the spring and summer, because the evaporation is much less.

In winter there should be no water left in the saucers; with the exception of aquatics, who require it

A small toy watering pot such as are sold for children's use, is of the greatest assistance; it will sprinkle the surface of tiny pots without wetting either stands or window glass.

A piece of oilcloth is an excellent protection to carpets, and should always be placed under every window and plant stand

It is best to select a cloudy day for giving your plants a thorough cleaning, thereby imitating nature, as she seldom washes her vegetation, with the sun shining upon it.

A pail of warm water can be brought into the parlor, and each plant thoroughly wetted in it, the surface of each leaf well moistened, without making any disturbance with the arrangement of the room.

Plants perspire like human beings, only the amount is seventeen times as great, according to Mr. Hale's computation

In the Hydrangea, the minute orifices in the space of an inch, are found to be one hundred thousand.

Protection from Frost.

During the winter our tender plants are liable to become frost-bitten in spite of every precaution we may take in their behalf. When the mercury out of doors settles to 25° and 30°, some little branches and leaves will droop, and the soil in some pots may become solid in doors.

If this happens, all is not lost. Take the blighted plants tenderly, and dip them into cold water, not icy cold, but drawn from hydrant or cistern; then place them in complete darkness where not a ray of light can penetrate, and in three days at the utmost, you will find them fresh as ever, every leaf upright and green, while if they had been left in the light, every leaf would have fallen. Several times we have had this experience with our plants and have always revived them

If the pots are set back at night from the windows on a piano or table, they will often escape freezing.

If a window opens on to a piazza, the plants can be protected by pinning a thick comforter outside of the window, or tucking it into the blinds.

Double windows are highly essential in a cold climate to keep off the intense cold, but they should always have an opening, a pane of glass with a hinge, or some means by which the room can be aired daily ; the weekly cleaning is not often enough to open the windows.

Do not forget to shade them from too much light and heat in the early part of the evening.

The great secret of success in window gardening, consists in overcoming as much as possible the disadvantages under which the plants labor, and rendering their position and treatment as much as possible like those growing in the open air.

Spring Culture of Window Gardens

March is the first month that treads upon the flowery border of spring; it is the beginning of the sunny season which shall awake the sleeping bulbs, plants, shrubs, and indeed all vegetation

March, April, May and June, are very busy months, for in them we make large additions to our collections of plants by propagating new varieties, both by seeds and cuttings.

WINDOW GARDENING.

Of course with all your fancy for new things, you will not forget to secure some few pots of good old fashioned flowers. They may be dear to many from only childish associations, having proved their value by the many years in which they have been cherished.

The culture in the spring months differs but little from that of the winter; more air can be given, and often the windows can be let down from the top for the whole day. Remember that if the thermometer stands at 55° and 65° out of doors, and the sun shines brightly, too much fresh air is impossible; but have the windows closed by three o'clock, for by that time a chilly wind often springs up in April, which would prove injurious to many tender plants, in a rapidly growing condition. Later in the season there is no danger. Great attention must be paid to general cleanliness; now is the season to promote rapid growth, but if the plants cannot breathe freely, they are in a decidedly consumptive state, and must pine away. To prolong the blooming of plants, every fading flower, even if it is but one in a cluster, should be cut away.

To keep the flowers of Azaleas from falling, it is an excellent plan to drop a single drop of gum water underneath the flower, where it sinks into the calyx; now is the time for their most profuse bloom, and they can be made more ornamental by this process.

No flowers should be left with water standing in their saucers, but if the plants are sunk in boxes or moss, there is no need of using saucers, which are hard to keep clean.

Be sure and attend to the weekly washing, it is quite as essential to your plants as to your household cleanliness

A small sized brush such as painters use, will be found of great service as it will wash off the tiniest leaf and stem.

Water must be given plentifully during the spring months, and it is well to supply it till a few drops ooze out from the bottom of the pot; but don't water while the sun shines full upon the plants.

Rain water is always the best for all vegetation. We especially recommend warm water in cold latitudes, as it cannot help but prove more invigorating to the roots. The sun does not shine every day; often it is withdrawn for a week, but if the soil is warmed with the water, it will not check the growth of the plants as much. This rule does not apply so closely to conservatories; there the plant can be sprinkled as though they were growing in the open ground, and warm water is not so much of a necessity in a greenhouse, where the whole temperature is adapted to the needs of plant-life. But this is not the case in window gardens, and we think its use the greatest benefit to them. Early in April, or in the later days of March, the plants that were stored in the cellar for safe keeping should be brought to the light; the decayed leaves and dust must be carefully brushed away and picked off, and the plant repotted, ready to start forth afresh.

The more hardy plants, like Roses, Geraniums, Pansies, etc., etc., can be put out of doors on warm days to enjoy an hour or so of fresh air and sunshine, at noontime; or if a warm rain falls, all the plants can go out and drink in fresh life with every drop. But don't let them remain out too long; a chill in April is often fatal to Heliotropes, variegated leaved plants, Fuchsias, etc. One must be governed by the climate

In March or April, according to your latitude, it is well to look into the subject of repotting the plants that have stood in the window. If the plants have had the requisite care and attention during the winter, they have made many new roots and must now have larger pots if you would have them grow to the best advantage.

Water the pots freely so that the ball of earth will slip out easily, and have your fresh potting soil moist to the touch. Never pot a plant with its ball of earth quite dry, for you cannot give it a good watering in that state. All the water you may supply will run down the fresh soil at the sides, and the plant will experience the fate of Tantalus of old, and literally starve to death, although its nourishment is in sight. If you use new pots, let them be soaked in water over night if possible, and at least three or four hours before using them. If your pots are old, let them be thoroughly washed, and cleansed from all green mould and soil.

It is not needful to provide larger pots when the first roots show themselves; but when they have twined and interlaced their tiny fibres, then they require more room. Often a light rap upon the edge of the pot, will be sufficient to turn out the ball of earth; but if not, a thin bladed knife can be run around close to the pot for an inch or two from the top, and this will bring it out easily. Turn it out with your hand and examine the roots; if they are closely curled about it, the plant requires a pot one size larger. Fill the pot with rich compost and put in the ball and plant directly in the centre, for a plant growing sideways in a pot looks very badly; fill up all around the sides of the pot, packing the soil down firmly with the fingers, cover the ball to the depth of a quarter or half an inch, leaving a vacant space of half an inch more to the edge of the pot for the purpose of watering to advantage.

When you turn out the plant, the roots will sometimes appear decayed, and the soil poor, dried, and gritty; then wash it all away, removing the dried roots, and give fresh, rich soil, pressing it firmly about the roots, but keep the same sized pot.

Perhaps you will find your plants injured by injudicious watering, the roots rotted, and the soil sodden. Cut off the roots as much as possible without removing the whole of them, and plant them in much smaller pots with a sandy soil, and they will regain their health.

As the weather grows warmer in May, many plants can be placed in balconies or on piazzas, and shielded from chilly winds and cold nights by mats or blankets, or they may be removed to cooler rooms where the sunshine will be sufficiently warm to keep them healthy. This is far better than roasting them in the hot rooms that many will live in, spite of all remonstrances to the contrary.

Sweet Verbenas should be brought from their winter quarters early in March, and they will soon put forth their light green, deliciously perfumed leaves.

WINDOW GARDENING

The plants that will flower most profusely in these months are :

Azaleas.	Heliotropes.
Abutilons.	Lantanas
Acacias.	Libonia floribunda.
Anemones.	Lobelias.
Auriculas.	Mahernia odorata.
Achimenes.	Maurandias.
Bouvardias.	Myrtles.
Begonias	Oranges.
Calla Aethiopica.	Oleanders.
Cinerarias.	Pelargoniums.
Cyclamens.	Primroses.
Daphnes.	Petunias.
Dielytra.	Pansies.
Epiphyllum Truncatum, etc.	Roses. Tea. Hybrids. Bourbons
Fuchsias.	Bengal Roses.
Gardenias.	Verbenas.
Geraniums, in all varieties.	Violets.

The Mush plant (*Mimulus moschatus*) is an universal favorite.

For culture in outside window boxes, the best are *Violets*, early flowering *Snow Drops*, early flowering *Anemones*, *Forget-me-Nots* and *Primroses*.

Summer Culture of Window Gardens.

June, July and August, do not require as much labor as the busy months of springtime. To be sure the cultivator needs to give daily attention lest the plants should become dried up from want of water; and must also tie, stake, prune, air, and weed with great care.

Water will now be required in greater quantities, and it need not be any warmer than standing in the sun will make it. The evening is the best time to apply it, because the plants will drink it up during the night to their great advantage, while if given in the morning, the sun's rays will claim their share, and, by quick evaporation much will be lost in the atmosphere. There are some plants that will desire, and must have water twice in the twenty-four hours. Fuchsias, Callas, Lobelias, etc., should have water both night and morning.

After the first of June, the plants will enjoy all the fresh air that can be given both night and day, in nearly all latitudes. Calceolarias and Cinerarias will be benefited by being kept cool, which can be done by placing them on damp moss, or refuse tan bark, and covering the surface of the pot with it. By the middle of June they can be placed in a cool, shady window, and all the stems that have flowered should be cut off, or if planted in a cool border, they will furnish more roots which can be divided in September or October.

By the end of May, in many localities, many plants will flourish better outside the window than inside; Geraniums, Pelargoniums, Fuchsias, Roses, Heliotropes, etc., etc., can be placed in boxes and vases on piazzas or balconies, or a garden can be made on the roof.

Large strong boxes can be attached to the outside of the windows, and all the plants set into them. In this way much care is avoided, for the plants can be watered with a syringe or watering pot, and the *debris* of withered leaves and stems is more easily cleared away. The plants can also be kept much freer from insects, and will grow more luxuriantly. Manure waterings can be given weekly. A tablespoonful of guano in a gallon of water, which should stand in the sun two or three days before being applied, is the easiest to procure, but all or any of the manures alluded to before, can be employed. When the flower buds appear, stimulants are much needed; and if no other can be procured, try this. Put a teaspoonful of *aqua ammonia* into a gallon of water, and sprinkle it all over the leaves and surface of the soil. Cut off all faded flowers; this greatly helps to keep the plants free from mildew, and increases their healthy condition; every yellow leaf should be taken off as soon as perceived.

If ever a plant becomes thoroughly dry from oversight or neglect, place it in a deep pan of rain water (if possible,) and let it remain for an hour or longer, until it is thoroughly soaked, but do not let the pot be entirely covered with the water. Hot water will frequently revive faded cut flowers; cut off a small bit of the stem, and then immerse the end into very hot water; you can see the petals smooth out from their crumpled folds, the leaves uncurl, and the whole branch and flower resume its beauty. Colored flowers revive the most completely. White flowers turn yellow, and the thickest textured petals come out the best from this hot foot bath

For preserving flowers in water, there is nothing so good as finely powdered charcoal. It keeps the water from all obnoxious odors. As a general rule too much air and too much light can not be given; yet when in full bloom the direct rays of the sun will cause delicate flowers to fade rapidly, while if they are shaded from the noon-tide heat, their beauty will be much prolonged; but during the night the more fresh air they breathe is the better.

If house-plants are plunged in pots into the borders, care must be taken to either close up the outlet at the botom of the pot, or else to put bits of plank or shingles under them, or set them upon small stones. This is needful on account of the tendency of their tiny rootlets to force their way out of the pot, and when the plant is removed, they must necessarily be cut off, thereby causing it to droop *or wither*, and greatly injuring its growth.

It is not advisable to let your plants run to seed. You desire to secure flowers, and to do this you must not let the plant fulfil its mission of leaves, buds, flowers and seeds in natural order, but by cutting off all the faded blooms, stimulate it to shoot forth fresh branches and buds, and strive to do its duty.

In order to secure seeds that are worth planting, it is needful to pick off all the later buds, and throw the whole strength of the plant into forming seed that will prove worth the raising.

Do not omit the practice of washing your pot plants in the summer, thinking that the rain will do it for you. It will help you doubtless, but if the leaves are bushy, many of them will not have their full share, and should still be syringed and washed with all the help of thumb and finger, sponge, brush, or garden syringe Keep the soil well stirred up in these months, for if you desire healthy plants the air must have access to the roots, and the surface of the pot must not be allowed to cake. There are many annuals that make fine pot plants both in summer and winter, but in June, July and August, they will give you most brilliant flowers at a very small cost. Boxes of Portulacca, Asters, Phlox, Stocks, Balsams, Pinks, Schizanthus, Zinnias, etc., are highly ornamental and within the reach of all flower lovers, while each of the above named flowers make handsome single plants in pots.

We can hardly give a list of flowers that bloom in these months, for their name is legion, and embraces many of those mentioned heretofore.

The Lilies are in their glory, and there can be no finer pot plants raised than the various varieties of Japan Lilies, Tigridias, Amaryllis and *Vallotta purpurea superba*, all of which are mentioned in the chapter upon bulbs.

Late in August, cuttings can be struck from all bedding-out plants that are desired to be kept during the winter. At this season they strike root very freely, and will frequently become fine plants by December.

Gloxinias and Achimenes are most desirable additions to summer blooming flowers. The Gloxinias are particularly beautiful and brilliant. Their exquisite coloring and freshness is unequaled.

Achimenes are, also, a genus of splendid plants, which will be described in Part II. They are unrivaled in beauty of coloring and form. They produce the most beautiful masses of blossoms in vases and baskets, over which they festoon their glorious flowers and trailing branches.

Autumn Culture of Window Gardens

For this season there is little to be added to the directions already given for the culture of house plants in previous months The plants that are intended for winter flowering should all be repotted and prepared for their permanent quarters early in September, so as to become fully established in the pots before the season is cold and gloomy. The roots must be attended to as heretofore directed, and if they cling to the surface of the pot, one of a larger size should be substituted, and fresh earth given. Be sure to procure good soil, and to press it tightly about the roots, and crown of the bulb, or stem of the plant

Do not attempt to cultivate too many plants, remembering that one strong, handsome shaped healthy plant is worth more than ten or twelve sickly things, that are lanky, scraggy and never blossom

Give your plants the morning sunshine. It is far better than the afternoon, and if the windows open, both to the east and southwest, so much the better for the plants at both windows; yet, if no other location can be procured, the afternoon sun is far better than none at all.

Never use glazed pots or crockery and painted ware, unless the common pots are set into them for ornamental purposes

Stimulate once a week with some one of the various liquid manures alluded to

Avoid extremes of cold and heat, and give all the air that is allowable, according to the temperature out of doors

Of course, each gardener must regulate her plants, according to the latitude in which she lives. If, on the Pacific slope, the dust that is so tenacious during summer and autumn must be the greatest enemy to contend with, while on the Atlantic coast the chilly, bleak east winds are the greatest drawbacks to successful plant culture. In the west, the cold winds blow from the Rocky Mountains.

No set code of rules can be given, and common sense must govern window gardening, as well as in all the branches of domestic economy.

A large sponge will do duty for a watering pot, or a hand brush broom dipped into water and shaken over the plants; but sprinkling must be given in some shape, at least, once a day.

If the pots are thoroughly washed with hot soap suds, all tendency to green mould will be prevented

Make the water that is given, warmer now than in the summer. Put your finger into the saucer, and see how cold it is, when it drains through the outlet. And if quite cold, give water of a greater warmth.

Plants that are in a state of rest, should have but very little water during the autumn.

Bulbs must be started for early flowering in September and for Easter, blooming late, in November.

Roses should all be repotted with rich soil: full two-thirds of entirely decomposed cow manure and leaf mould, so decayed as to crumble in the fingers, should be added, to one-third of good sandy loam.

As most of the desirable flowering plants will be treated of in their respective chapters, it will only be a repetition to notice them here, or to give a list of them

CHAPTER V.

INSECTS, AND HOW TO KILL THEM.

The previous anxieties of the gardener are but light compared to the deadly warfare he is now forced to wage against the tiny insects which not only infest his house-plants, but the soil in which they grow and bloom.

The red spider is the most minute, yet the most dangerous foe wherewith we have to deal. Hot and close parlors and sitting-rooms, are its delight, and it weaves its tiny webs about the casements waiting until the plants are ready to feed it.

He is a treacherous invidious enemy seeming to lie in the window frames quiet and warm, but ready to seize upon our rarest Roses, most valuable Fuchsias and Carnations, as soon as they are placed in their winter quarters.

It is the tiniest of red mites; the merest grain as it lies in repose under the leaves of the plant it has chosen for its dwelling, but when the leaf is closely examined, it rushes wildly about, apparently knowing that it is doomed, and its minutes are numbered

Though these pests are so minute, one can easily discover their presence; for the upper sides of the leaves grow brown and sire, and the plant loses its healthy appearance.

A thorough sprinkling and washing may drive away the intruders, but if the heated and close atmosphere is still continued, plenty more will be generated.

Red pepper has been found decidedly obnoxious to it. It should be dusted upon with a pepper castor, holding the plant bottom side upwards, while another person dusts on the pepper. Of course you must take care not to let it fall in any quantity upon the soil of the pot, lest it should injure the roots.

A decoction of quassia will also act fatally upon insect life, if used in the following proportions:

Boil one ounce of quassia wood in three pints of water until but a quart remains; when luke warm, either dip in the infested plants, or sponge off each leaf with a sponge or brush. Let them stand fifteen minutes or so, then dip the plants or wash them off with clear water, as the decoction of quassia, if allowed to remain on the leaves, will injure them.

Tobacco smoke is also a good preventive to some insects, but this red spider does not seem to heed it.

The *aphis* or green fly, does not affect a liking for tobacco, for it intoxicates it, and causes it to fall from the leaves and branches of all plants. Hold a lighted cigar under the leaves of your Roses, etc., not so near as to curl them with the heat however, and see how they will fall down completely stupefied; but, if left to themselves, they will revive, and slowly return to their leafy homes. Place a paper under the leaves when you apply the smoke, and then you can easily destroy them.

If a plant is very much infested with these noxious pests, take the pot in your hand and spread a paper under it, then with a feather or small wing, brush off the insects and burn them all up. Then dip the plant into warm water, to kill the eggs, and with a weekly washing, smoking or sprinkling, not an insect will be seen.

A conservatory plant-stand, or window garden with plants covered with these insects, plainly announces the neglect they have received. The old maxim seems to come here again in play, *i. e.* "An ounce of prevention is worth a pound of cure."

If plants were as carefully washed and tended as many pet animals were, there would be no need of any remedies against insects.

Conservatories can be kept free of all insects by being smoked once a week with tobacco. Close all the windows carefully that lead into the house, take the largest size flower pot-saucer, put a shovel full of blazing coals into it, and pour over them an ounce of tobacco, letting it smoke well; if it is slightly dampened the smoke will be more dense. Let it smoke for half an hour, then open the window out of doors, and let the smoke go out. Choose a bright fair day when half an hour's outside air will not injure the plants, and you will keep all of them fresh and vigorous.

The *mealy bug*, is a white mealy looking insect, but very destructive to plant life. It does not dislike tobacco, but has a hatred to whale oil soap. A quarter of a pound dissolved in five quarts of water, and syringed on to the plants, or sprinkled with a watering pot, will force it to disappear.

Like the aphis, it can be brushed off with a chicken's wing.

Brown scale will sometimes attack Roses, Daphnes, Oranges and Pittosporums, but it is not nearly as common as the above mentioned insect. Bad ventilation and dark places are its chief cause and *habitat ;* frequent washings and picking off with the hand, are its only means of destruction, as it thrives on tobacco smoke, and makes no objection to the disgusting odor of whale oil soap suds.

Thrips is a dark brown or whitish yellow fly, very active on the wing, and greatly injurious to many plants. It will not thrive where tobacco smoke is given to plants, and is most likely to be found where plants are placed thickly together, in a shaded window.

The *Verbena mite* is a most tiny insect, smaller than the red spider, and quite as disastrous in its ravages. It cannot be seen with the naked eye, but viewed through a microscope, it appears as large as a house fly

If it attacks your plants, it appears like a black rust so thickly does it congregate together. It delights in Heliotropes, Petunias, Verbenas, etc., and is closely allied to the insect which infests the Plum, Peach and Cherry trees

Neither sulphur, tobacco, or whale oil soap are obnoxious to it, but it will run away from the "Grafton Mineral Fertilizer," and a thorough sprinkling of the dry powder on the leaves or stems well moistened, will make the insects dislodge their hold, not to return.

There is another mite whose color varies from green to black, and is as particular in its attentions to Carnations and Pinks, and so rapid in its movements, that it has been named the "Carnation Twitter." It is very destructive to all the varieties of plants above mentioned, and it affects the leaves like the spider, making them very unhealthy in appearance and as yet no means have been found to destroy it.

If plants grow vigorously, are healthy and well cared for, the ravages of insects are not to be much dreaded; and if they do appear they can be quickly routed. Undoubtedly we must fight if we would become the owners of handsome, finely formed, profuse blossoming plants; and she who devotes the most time to them, will be the proudest of the flowers she rears.

Sulphur and tobacco are powerful remedies in the hands of an amateur, and will often not only kill all the insects, but destroy all the plants. As almost every amateur usually undertakes to try some experiment for himself, so we record the experience of a lady who writes us :

"Years ago, when we had the charge of a small conservatory, we tried the effect of sulphur thrown upon hot coals to kill infested plants. Every insect succumbed before its direful fumes; so also did the plants; hardly a leaf remained on the stems the following day, and the poor leafless branches spake to me in terms of sad reproach through their mute lips. I was then a tyro in the business, and greatly desired to have every thing done *thoroughly*.

"Thus I learned, that there is no teacher like experience, his school is a hard one, he is a stern disciplinarian, but when his lessons are once learned they are not forgotten, but are indelibly printed upon the pages of memory

"Luckily for my conservatory, it was denuded of its leaves in May, and soon the poor forlorn plants were set out into the borders where they could recuperate and regain the foliage denuded by so strong a sulphur bath.

"Again: I tried tobacco tea, and in it steeped each treasured Rose, each loved Fuchsia, and they looked so worn and weary after it that I was heart sick with my efforts in their behalf. Since then, I have been very shy of trying such experiments, and content myself with hand brushing and washing, but still more with the daily care, the constant loving attention which is much the surest and the safest for flowers."

White mites may frequently be seen infesting the soil in pots. They seem to be the larvæ of a small black or brown fly, and are very injurious to the well-being of the plants. Lime water, salt and water, and hot water, have all been tried. The first two were inefficient to injure them, and the last killed the plants. Now we turn in a goodly supply of warm water, and when we see wriggling specks of white, take up the pot and turn off the water. Give another supply, and turn that away, and continue to do so until not one remains. The third or fourth day the process is repeated, and by this means the troublesome mites are destroyed

Wood ashes will sometimes drive them away. They appear to be on or near the surface of the pot. Red pepper carefully dusted over the outside of the earth will kill them, and then the earth containing it can be removed, lest the pepper might prove too heating to the roots. Salt is said to drive them away. We tried it as recommended, and killed half a dozen of our finest Carnations, so concluded not to try such rash experiments on choice plants. Again, in using the red pepper, of course you must not put on a full spoonful, but only a slight sprinkling over the surface, where the worms lie the thickest.

If angle worms are in the soil, they can be removed by turning out the ball of earth and picking them out, and if a fine hair pin or knitting needle is thrust into the soil, they will all come to the surface and can easily be dislodged.

Lime water will also drive them out and help the growth of the plant, keeping the foliage fresh and bright. It can be applied once a week without damage to the plant, and can be made by slacking a small piece of fresh lime in hot water, then adding cold, and stirring it well. The water will only dissolve just so much lime, and the residue will remain in the pail or firkin used to dissolve it. More water can be turned on to it, and so continue until it is all taken up. Then bottle the water and cork up for use. Keep the bottles where they will not freeze. A little of the undissolved lime can be put into every bottle, and when the water turns out discolored, more can be added to it.

A tablespoonful of spirits of camphor, added to a pint and a half of water, will make a good wash to keep off insects. But with proper care and good management these antidotes need not be employed.

Fresh water well applied, fresh air at proper times, and cleanliness at all times, are the best preventives one can employ against insects.

CHAPTER VI.

Propagation from Seeds, Cuttings, etc.

At present most of our Window Gardens in cities are filled with plants bought from the florist. Of course one half do not know how they are grown, and hence do not well know how to take care of them.

Every window gardener, it seems to us, should understand the first principles of plant life, and learn for himself how they are propagated.

Nearly all plants that are desirable for window gardening can be raised either from seeds, cuttings or by grafting. Bulbous roots are propagated chiefly from offsets, and the new varieties are produced from the seeds. Other plants are also increased by offsets or separating the roots, but their number is comparatively few.

Warmth, moisture, proper temperature and a soil suitable to promote the sprouting of the germ, and a shady situation until the seeds have swelled, are essential to the vegetation of seeds.

For window plants a greater degree of warmth is needful. Unless the air is from 66° to 70°, and some bottom heat is supplied, your success will not satisfy you. Seeds of tender plants require hot house treatment. Moisture must not be with held at any time; yet, if it is in excess, the seeds are apt to decay before they sprout. A thick piece of flannel wet with hot water, and laid over the soil and pressed lightly down upon it, will ensure the needful moisture, warmth and darkness. Warm water should be given over it, letting it permeate slowly through it. It must be lifted daily to see if the tender seeds are starting; the flannel must be removed before the leaves appear, and a pane of glass which will exactly cover the seed box or pot placed closely over them.

Too deep planting is a fruitful cause of failure with amateur seed raisers. The depth of the soil must be proportioned to the size of the seed. Petunias, Primulas, etc., require the least sprinkling of sandy loam.

A good general rule is to cover the seed only to the thickness of their own diameter, yet this would not hold good with Sweet Peas, for they grow better when planted three inches in depth.

With very fine seeds it is best to press them lightly into the surface of the soil with the fingers, then shade from the sun three or four days either with cloth or newspapers, and sprinkle over the coverings, not letting them become dry at all, rot not killing the germ of the seeds by too much water.

Most plants fail by sowing their seeds in soil that is too wet or too dry. All seeds sown in pots are more difficult to manage than those raised in a hot bed or in the border on account of the danger of drying up. The ancient maxim again comes up, "that if a thing is worth doing at all, it is worth doing well." So in plant culture it is just as easy to do it right as wrong. The soil should be light and sandy; clear sand, such as the masons use for making plaster, is just the thing with which to cover the seeds, and to mix with the loam. The soil should not be all of sand, because it will dry too quickly. Nor must it be of clayey loam, because it will keep too wet, and will not let the air circulate freely enough to make the seeds vegetate. But a good loam mixed with sand will answer our purpose exactly.

Fill the pots with it and leave quarter of an inch of clear, sand at the top, for the minute seeds, and half an inch for those of larger size. Abutilons, Pelargoniums, Coboea, etc. Set the pots in water up to the rims to let the soil become thoroughly wetted, then place them to drain for half an hour or more. Plant the seeds on the surface, sprinkling over them and pressing lightly upon them sand proportionate to their needs.

The sand must not be allowed to dry at all, and we find that nearly all kinds of seeds will germinate more quickly in it than in loam, though a mixture of both may be desirable in some cases when the care is not constant. Shallow cigar boxes are preferable to pots; they will hold much more, can be handled as easily, and make the best seed pans that we know of.

The soil for planting seeds should be as fine as possible. It is a good plan to bake it in an old pan in the oven, then sift it through a good sized sieve, which can be made out of an old milk pan, by boring holes through the bottom of it. Soil thus prepared is far better than if taken directly from the garden, yet in all cases it is better to buy it of the florists, then you know it is just right.

When the second tier of leaves show themselves, it is time to transplant the seedlings, into the pots or boxes in which you intend them to grow and bloom.

There is some art in watering seedlings as well as plants, as there is great danger of the tiny sprouts becoming water clogged or "damped off."

It is often better to water little pots by placing them in shallow pans of water, and letting them suck up moisture for a few minutes. Boxes can be moistened by pouring the water against the sides of them, holding the spout close to them, and letting only a small stream fall from the nozzle, thus gently wetting the whole surface.

The pane of glass that is to be kept over the young plants, can be edged upon one side to give more air, and prevent their growing spindling, and wire drawn.

Bell glasses are much better however, and are largely used in England and in France where they are called *cloches*. They are conical, rising to a sharp point in the middle, and are of cheap construction. Seedlings raised under them flourish finely, and there is little need for watering tiny plants; for when the edge of the glass is within the rim of the pot, the moisture becomes condensed upon the sides of the glass, and moistens the soil by trickling down upon it.

WINDOW GARDENING. 51

Another desirable way is to pack the pot in which the seeds are planted, into another pot of larger size, and fill up the space with moss, refuse hops or tan bark, which can be kept both warm and moist with hot water. A little of it can stand in the saucer which holds the largest pot, and thus a uniform state of moisture can be preserved.

Hard shelled seeds, like Canna, Acacias, Cypress Vines, etc., will germinate much quicker if they are soaked in boiling water for an hour or so. Turn it upon them boiling hot, and let it stand until cool, then plant the seeds. Some gardeners prefer to pour boiling water upon the surface of the soil prepared for them, rather than upon the seeds. Either way will succeed, but it is essential to soften the horny substance which envelops the seeds, if you desire them to grow.

Verbena seeds require soaking in warm water over night; turn the water upon them, and let the cup stand in a warm place.

Many beautiful plants can be raised from seeds as easily as from cuttings, and be more highly appreciated because they are all your own, developed by your patient care and attention.

Begonias, Callas, Oleanders, Cyclamens, Calceolarias, Gloxinias, Primulas, Carnations, Lantanas, Coleus, Heliotropes, Geraniums, Cinerarias, Pelargoniums, Camellias, Abutilons and Cacti, etc., can all be made to grow into fine plants, but it requires constant care and patience to cultivate them.

Some of them are very long in germinating, others in blooming, and they require much time, for the least neglect will often prove fatal to them.

Cuttings.

There is little trouble raising plants from cuttings; a few rules are essential, and a little care and time are requisite, but any one can make them strike root.

They can be struck either from woody pieces without leaves, but all ready to send them forth, or from young green shoots.

The first mentioned will rarely fail to grow, but they grow slowly, taking sometimes a long time to start the first leaf, while the nice green shoots will quickly become respectable plants. But it is well to know that if the branches of an old plant are broken down, the hard woody stems will produce in time, fine plants.

Take a hard old stem of Geranium, Fuchsias, Myrtle, Heliotrope, Sweet Verbena, or any desirable plant, and cut it so as to leave one or two joints or eyes on a piece, (a joint is the slight thickening of the branch whence the leaves and side branches will come out), set them into a damp sponge or moss, keeping it moistened, for four or five days, a week may not be too long, but keep them in a dark cool place. A slight callous will then be formed, and the cutting will be all ready to put forth fresh roots as soon as it is potted.

In carrying cuttings from place to place, it is best to wrap them in a damp sponge, leaving out the upper leaves, and covering the sponge with oil silk or enamel cloth. All cuttings strike root more quickly in sand than in loam, and i the bottom of the joint touches the side of the pot or box, it hastens its growth. Bottom neat is quite as needful to propagate cuttings as seeds, and the heated cases referred to in another chapter would give every amateur a desirable hot bed at a slight outlay. To raise cuttings from a fresh or succulent branch, it is needful to take one in a proper condition to secure success.

Mr. Henderson says, that if a cutting bends, it will not grow easily, but if it snaps off it is ready to make root, and become a vigorous plant. This test does not always apply to woody stemmed plants like Myrtles, Sweet Verbenas, Daphnes, Roses and Azaleas, but their growth is usually finer if the wood is easily broken.

Whether the cuttings are of hard or succulent growth, they are similarly planted, and they can be inserted all around the edge of a pot not over an inch apart, and nearly as deep as the second eye.

CHAPTER VII.

Propagating Boxes, Heating Cases and Cold Frames.

There are always some plants that are very difficult to start without some bottom heat, and all amateur gardeners cannot possess a hot bed. But the heated case affords to them the greatest facilities for striking cuttings, raising seeds, and bringing well established plants into rapid growth.

A home made case may be made in the form of a double cube, say twelve inches wide and high, and eighteen inches long. A concealed tank of zinc filled with hot water, will give out and retain the heat from twelve to twenty-four hours without changing the water. No lamp or extra heat need be used, and the cases are perfectly clean and unobjectionable, while they can be with a little mechanical skill, rendered very ornamental and agreeable objects for any parlor or sitting room.

It is best that the entire frame work be made of wood, and the sides and top consist each of a pane of glass fitted into the frame; or in other words, it is a small glass show case with open bottoms. One of the sides may be arranged so as to slide out to give greater ease in arranging the plant within and for cleaning the glass. The top may be movable, fastened by hinges, and lifted up one or two inches occasionally for ventilation. When the plants are in bloom, the entire side or top can be left open all day.

The wood work may be either painted or be constructed simply of black walnut, oak, and oiled; either will look well.

In some of our horticultural stores there are cases already constructed for propagating purposes which fill the exact need.

Figs. 17 and 18 are manufactured of galvanized iron, one being about three feet

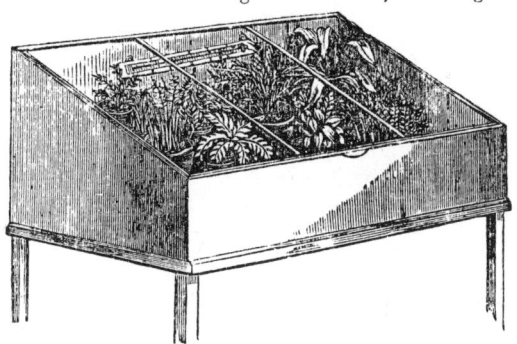

Fig. 17.

long and two wide, the other one foot by eighteen inches   A shallow boiler about the size of the bottom is fitted in each case, filled with water, and heated by the flame of either a lamp or gas jet beneath. The top is of glass and can be lifted at any time fresh air is needed. A thermometer completes the equipment. It is very simple and successful. The heat can be run up to any desired point and the lady who uses it can soon initiate herself into the mysteries and practice of rooting, cutting and propagating fine bedding plants.

Fig. 19 is a propagating box made of earthen ware, with grooves in the top for a pane of glass to slide up and down with a cover. The heat thus generated can be retained for a considerable length of time by closing the glass top. They are very suitable for starting soft wooded cuttings in sand.

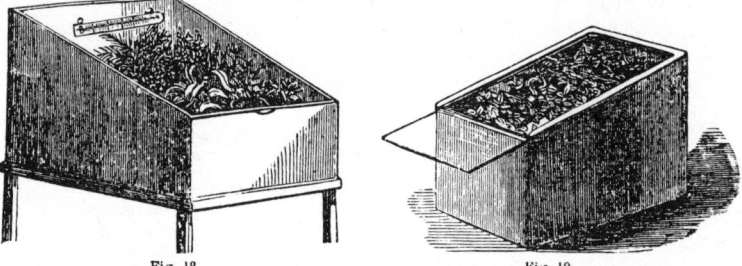

Fig. 18.   Fig. 19.

A forcing stand may be erected like this in Fig. 20. It consists of a wrought iron frame of ornamental design with two stories. In each story there is a row of double pans, the bottom one containing water which is heated by a patent kerosene lamp, keeping the temperature of the inner pan about 100°. In this inner pan are placed mould, sand or loam, wherein the pots are plunged. The heat of the water is communicated directly through the sand to the cutting or seeds which will germinate in a few days.

All cultivators need to know that for propagating purposes, there is needed heat and moisture, and to be successful you need a greater bottom heat than surface heat, and also, still, quiet atmosphere.

If this case is used in a room where the temperature is usually quite mild, no glass covering will be needed; still if it is needed, a case like that described in the former part of this chapter may be constructed for each shelf. If pots are used in these little cases, they should be very small, not over two inches in diameter.

Fig. 20.

Such little contrivances as these render it comparatively easy for any lady to raise her own Verbenas, Pelargoniums, or other simple plants, and would undoubtedly do more to please and instruct children and visitors, by way of amusement, than the whole apparatus originally cost.

In spring, which is the time that artificial heat will be most required, the zinc reservoirs of your propagating boxes will need to be filled with water, both night and morning. In cases like our first mentioned one, not heated with the lamp, boiling water should be used, and the temperature in the closed case will vary from 60° to 75°; the silver sand as soon as it becomes a little moist, heats the soil in the pots, and the heat is retained for a long time, often 24 hours after the tank was first filled.

Another home made case is constructed out of an old tea chest; cut it down about one third, then fit into it a zinc pan 4 to 5 inches in depth to hold the water, over the top put a large pane of glass, and in such a box, large numbers of cuttings may be raised with much less trouble than a hot bed causes. It can be kept in a back room or in the attic, and filled with small pots of cuttings and seeds. The glass top may be hinged on. But the best designs are, however, thus illustrated in Figs. 17, 18, and 19.

Cold Frames

Many plants that have grown out of doors all summer, and may be needed for blooming in the window during the winter and spring, may be safely housed in cold frames. This is a very desirable method for keeping a large quantity of plants.

A frame may be made very easily and cheap as follows: Take a sheltered location, protected from the north wind, and well drained, dig down four feet by eight—or four by twelve is a convenient size.

Insert at each corner scantling posts, rising six inches above the surface in front, and eighteen inches above at the rear; nail boards to the inside of these posts, leaving about six inches space between them and the earth, to be filled with manure or tan.

Outside the posts nail boards above the ground, leaving a space to be filled up with tan, etc.

Cover the top with double sashes. Fill in the bottom of the pit with small stones, or bits of charcoal, and throw in a foot or more of tan in which to sink the pots. Coal ashes will do as well as tan; they are required to secure dryness, warmth and ventilation.

When the cold weather comes on, cover the sashes with straw mats or carpeting—and bank up the pit with tan or manure—put a good embankment about the whole pit.

Place the plants in the pit, in the autumn, and let them have as much air as possible in mild days, covering closely, in cold nights.

The chief care is to give fresh air in sufficient quantities, and to protect in severe weather from frosts.

Roses, Geraniums, Salvias, Fuchsias, Heliotropes, etc. can be kept quite safely in such a pit, and be ready to force in the windows or conservatory by March

When warm days occur the sashes can be uncovered, and the sun allowed to shine through the glass on to the plants, but until February it is better to keep them in darkness, and not admit fresh air oftener than once in two or three weeks. Do it when the air is most genial, and raise the sashes only long enough to inspect the plants, and if very dry give a little water.

CHAPTER VIII.

Window Pots, Boxes, Jardinieres, and Plant Stands.

Glazed pots are not as good to grow plants in as the real pottery, on account of their want of porosity, which is a great help in watering, evaporation and aeration; likewise their saucers are sometimes fastened to them, and are liable to fill with earth, clog up the outlets, and are not easily cleaned.

The earthen pots are easily cleaned and plants thrive much better in them, than in fancy china or glass ones. Still these last are often desirable for room decoration, and many very handsome ones are made, which can be used by simply setting the other common pot in-

Fig. 21.

side, and if there is any vacant space between, it may be filled up with moss.

The size of the pot should be in unison with the size of the plant; the most convenient ones to handle, may measure from five to seven or eight inches across top. Yet it any have extensive window gardens, they will need all sizes. from 3, 4, 5, and 6 inches diameter, up to eight inches—some for propagating purposes, others for shifting into, from smaller sizes. Saucers of course, of the proper sizes, should fit each pot.

A new pot should be placed in a pail of water to soak, and expel the dry air from the pores, and an old pot should be carefully washed both inside and out before use. Pieces of charcoal broken up fine should be put into the bottom of each pot to the depth of about two or three inches; less of course in the smaller sized pots

Fig. 22.

As the pots become filled with roots, the plants must be shifted into a size larger, and when these are filled, again repotted into others.

Fig. 23.

Fig. 24.

It is easy to find when to repot the plants, by running a broad bladed table knife around the inner edge of the pot, and turning it bottom side upwards over the hand; the ball of earth readily slips out, and the roots are disclosed to view. If you suspect there are worms in the soil, their presence can be detected, by the fact that they soon come to the surface to know the cause of the disturbance, and then they can be destroyed.

The soil should be frequently stirred about the surface of the pots, and for this purpose a good sized hair pin or two-tined fork are good instruments. The for-

Fig. 25.

Fig. 26.

mer is best as its prongs are so small, raking up the earth without disturbing greatly the tiny rootlets.

In potting or repotting it is needful sometimes to cut back the plants, and when it is done, due deference must be paid to their shape, thinning out the branches so that they will be in good form, for the beauty of the plant is greatly dependent upon this.

Figs. 21 & 22 are very neat pots made of pottery ware nearly white, glazed on the outside, and intended to hold inside the common pots of earthen ware. Most of the florists have them as they are quite ornamental and are becoming popular. Their price is from $1.50 to $2.50.

An objection has been raised to the common pots, that they soon become dirty and covered with mould and rust, and need considerable care to keep clean. The only remedy is constant scrubbing. And it is impossible to have a thoroughly porous well drained pot, without its sides becoming in time old and sour; attempts have been made to paint them with ochre, or red whitewash, but it soon rubs off and is disagreeable. To combine ornament with use, the one must be placed inside the other.

Fig. 27.

There is a style of mountable flower pot, now used somewhat by English florists, made of separate slabs of wood joined together with flexible hinges. (See Fig. 23.) The advantages claimed for it, are that it can be taken to pieces and adjusted, that plants can be easily transplanted without disturbing the soil or injuring the roots. With small window gardens it would not be needed; but in the case of very large conservatory plants, where a diameter of two feet

Fig. 28.

is required it might be found useful, as the plant might need examination to perfect the drainage, or remove the soil and replace with fresh compost. The wires, as shown in the engraving, are moved down or up for tightening or loosening, so that any one can make them. There are several styles of pots, square, and made of prettily ornamented pieces of wood, (Figs. 25 & 26,) so simple that they need no explanation. The same designs have been copied in glazed ware with various colors and are accessible to any one who will visit the horticultural stores, or those places where the most tasteful pottery and household ware is kept for sale.

60 WINDOW GARDENING.

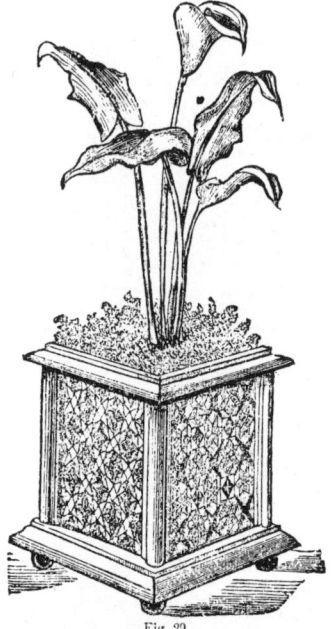

Fig. 29.

Fig. 30.

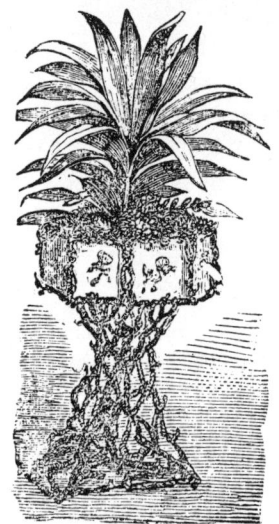

Fig. 31.

Fig. 32.

WINDOW GARDENING.

An exceedingly ornamental design for a flower pot for a drawing room is shown in (Fig. 27,) made of Minton tile, the ground work of which is dark blue and the flowers white. All such decorative pots impart a pleasant tasteful look to any room. We would be glad to have them multiplied and constantly improved Fig. 28, is of the same material, but of various shades of white, red and green.

Jardinieres.

These are fanciful, single or double boxes, of more artistic construction than the common pot, and intended to be used for decoration purposes entirely. Many are constructed and filled with entirely artificial moss, and imitation plants with highly colored leaves, are set therein. Of course little or no interest is felt in them after they have been placed in their position, while if they had been natural living plants, the very care they daily required would have developed far more love and appreciation than the former; still we would not omit either, all do well in their proper place.

Fig. 33.

Fig. 34.

Figs. 28 to 34, are rare ornaments of beauty, especially 29, 30, 32, which are exquisite in their rich coloring and material. They are constructed of glass mosaics, and intended to contain pots of choice plants, hidden with moss, and thus prepared to adorn the window of the drawing room or library. The glass mosaic is arranged in designs of richest colors, set into cement of pure white color, and the whole hardened and polished to one glistening surface. Some of the designs are imitations of snow crystals, and of course are the perfection of art. The interior of these pots is lined with zinc, and they may at will hold either plants with earth, or be filled with moss and hold cut flowers. The illustrations are taken from originals exhibited at one of the Crystal Palace exhibitions in London.

Figs. 31, 33, & 34, are sketches of other designs of rustic stands and boxes, with the Dracaena, which is a favorite with all fond of the plant decorations of

WINDOW GARDENING.

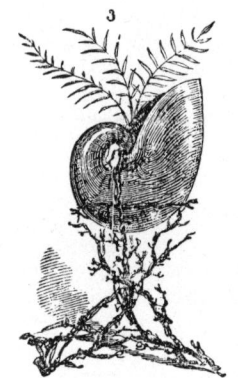

Fig. 35.

rooms. No. 34, is a rustic Tile Jardinet, hexagon shaped and 11 to 16 inches in diameter. No. 31, is the same mounted upon a rustic cedar wood stand. No. 33, is a china flower vase with fence pattern, made entirely round, and from 6 to 14 inches in diameter. No. 35, is a pretty little idea of a sea shell, fitted to a rustic frame; the interior of the shell is filled with compost or moss, and from it grows a feathery fern. No. 36, is a rustic wood basket, made by any one with a taste for mechanical construction and very simply put together. It is suitable for any house, and adapted to any position out doors or in doors. Will look best if filled with ferns, but when bulbs are in season, fill it with good selection of Hyacinths, Tulips or Crocuses, according to the fancy of the fair gardener. No. 37, is a rustic vase of circular outline, intended especially for indoor decoration They are very cheap; both should be lined with zinc, or else the presence of the damp earth will cause them to rot. When bulbs are past their spring blooming, then take Ferns or Dracaena, or any plant provided it is not of too great height, and must have an agreeable shading of color, with appropriate form and contour.

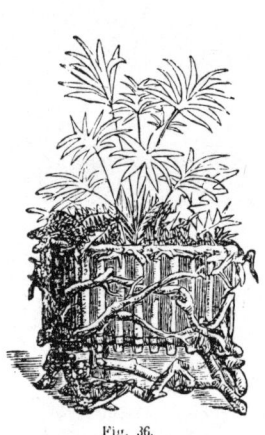
Fig. 36.

Fig. 37.

A large number of vari-colored floral pots and jardinieres, made of lava, and now imported from Europe, can be found of various prices from $1.50 to $5.00, in any of our fancy china ware and porcelain stores. They are of beautiful finish, and usually very cheap.

Some American manufacturers are now producing designs in terra cotta which are pleasing. Fig. 40, is used both as a hyacinth or bulb pot, or as a bouquet holder, the interior being previously filled with sand. The sizes vary from twelve to eighteen inches high, and consist of from three to five apertures for placing the bulb. They are usually well drained beneath.

Fig. 39, is a rustic pot of about nine inches high, resting upon a dolphin base six inches high. The sides of the pot are ornamented with a grape vine running around, and clusters of leaves and fruit.

Fig. 38, is a wall ivy basket about eight inches high, and proportionate height, intended to hold earth and a plant of Ivy, which will grow and clamber up either the sides of the room, or over the door if the pot is hung near. Two pots of the same design, might be very appropriately hung, one on each side of a window out doors, and the Ivy as it grew, be trained gracefully over the sides and top or the front of the house

Fig. 38

Window Boxes.

If the window should happen to be in a recess, the sills may be occupied with boxes. Almost anything will do if clean. A wooden trough lined with lead or zinc, may be constructed to hold a considerable quantity of earth, and here climbing plants may grow and root, and be trained in profusion over the entire window The Cobœa is often used for this purpose, and after it has

Fig. 39.

Fig. 40.

grown enough to fill the whole window, it may be allowed to hang down in festoons, forming a natural and graceful screen in any sunny window. Climbing vines need considerable care and examination, for they are apt to harbor spiders and insects of various descriptions. Likewise, they drop their dead leaves and flowers, necessitating constant cleanliness. Nothing is so clean and satisfactory as the Ivy. Everything in these pots must be regularly watered, and like all other pots, precaution must be had as to drainage; all troughs or boxes without exception should be lined with zinc

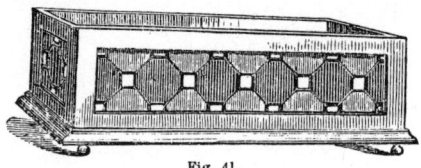

Fig. 41.

Fig. 41 is a design of a window box, constructed by an ordinary carpenter. Two boards of common timber eight inches wide, half an inch thick, and three and a half feet long, form the side of the box; the ends are twelve inches wide eight inches high, six and a half inches broad. The bottom board is twelve inches wide, one inch thick, three and a half feet long, and projects about an inch beyond the side all around. A tray or lining of zinc was made by the tinman and fitted in. A piece of oil cloth with a pretty pattern, and some mosaic tile work was obtained at the carpet store, and tacked carefully to the sides. Mouldings of wood were nailed all round the top, bottom and end, then all the wood work was stained by rubbing it over with burnt umber and water, and after it was dry, a coating of varnish was put on to finish it.

For filling such a box there is a great variety to choose from; at one time you may use Begonias, at another, Geraniums, with variegated foliage, such as the L'elegante. Then at your pleasure you may, in cool weather, change to young evergreens, of which Arbor Vitaes, twelve inches high, make the most cheerful appearance. During the winter time if you have it in a reasonably warm room, you can place several Dracaenas, the *D. terminalis* and *D. Australis* being the best

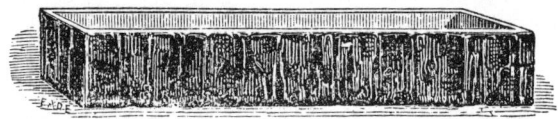

Fig. 42.

Fig. 42 is of plain tile or glazed earthenware.

Fig. 43, is of Minton tile more highly decorated, and costing about $15.00. The third or Fig. 44, is still more elegant, and represents it as it would appear filled with Bulbs, Hyacinths, Crocuses and Tulips.

The use of these costly window tile boxes is becoming more general every

year, and tradesmen inform us that the past year alone the demand in this country for these objects of taste has completely trebled.

Boxes made of plain wood may be ornamented with acorns, as shown in Fig 45, a design often used for green-houses or staircase windows. Take a mixture of acorn and powdered shells, cut all the acorns in half, lengthways, cover the box with glue, then lay the acorns flat side down along the edge and bottom of the sides, one after the other, and in the open space between, affix them in any fantastic plan you like; then sift the powdered shell thickly all over the box between the acorns, and it will soon dry. If you choose, you can vary the

Fig. 43.

acorns with cone seeds, and red berries cut in half. Another style, Fig. 46, is made in a similar way, excepting only that pine cones are used in place of acorns, and the edges of the box and its ends, and supports at bottom, are constructed of rustic cedar wood. This pot is filled with a fine collection of Bulbs, Hyacinths, Narcissus, Jonquils, Tulips, Crocuses, Snow Drop and Scillas, length about three feet, and width about eight inches.

There are other very pretty rustic modes of construction. The outside of home made boxes, may also be ornamented with white and gray lichens, wet in water to make them pliable, then glued on, or fastened securely with thread wire, attaching the wire to small brad nails on the inside and outer edge of the box.

Fig. 44.

When dry it will have a pleasing appearance. Sections of bark may also be used to cover the sides, or wood mosaic introduced; take the split half of small sticks of spruce, maple, oak and birch, arrange them in alternate diamonds, oval and square, varying the colors with an artistic eye, and fastening the cleft sticks with small brads, which will not be perceptible. When finished, cover with a coat of varnish.

Gum shellac, dissolved in turpentine, or common furniture polish may be used for varnishing. Pine cones are favorites in these box decorations, and sometimes are used either whole or are pulled to bits and nailed in regular rows along the boards

The preparation of these boxes for plants must be good; place, first a layer of finely powdered charcoal an inch in thickness over the bottom. It acts not only as a preventive against mould, but also as a fertilizer, enriching the soil Then select your compost, which has been previously described, composed of rich loam, sand and forest leaf mould, and decayed barn-yard manure, and fill up to the brim.

If you are growing bulbs leave out all manures, and use more leaf mould; see that the bottom of the box has means of drainage by a hole, into a saucer or dish to receive surplus water.

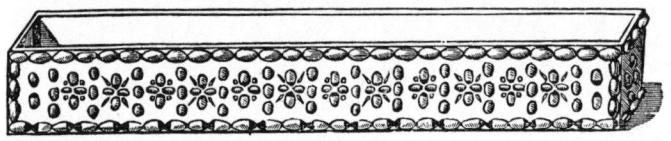

Fig. 45.

In arranging your plants give due heed to height and coloring. The flowers which grow the tallest must have the central position, and the dwarfs occupy the edges and corners. For drooping vines select the Money-wort, it grows freely, and its bright yellow flowers are very attractive. The *Partridge Vine*, which grows so plentifully in all the woodlands, is also desirable, its coral red berries adding greatly to its beauty. The variegated and green "Coliseum Ivy," is

Fig. 46.

good for this purpose. German and English Ivies are very valuable, growing with great rapidity, the former often two or three inches a day. The Convolvulus possesses bright green foliage and exquisite flowers; it is always a favorite in window gardening.

The *Cranberry Vine* has been overlooked, and deserves especial recommendation, both for window boxes and hanging baskets Its prettily cut foliage, pure white flowers, and rich scarlet berries, make it very ornamental; it is easily obtainable by any one.

For a good selection to fill one box for winter blooming, we would proceed as follows:

Place in the centre a winter blooming *Fuchsia*, either *Speciosa* with its pink waxen petals, and brilliant crimson corolla, which will bloom ten months in the year, or *Serratifolia*, with its corolla and petals of two shades of crimson.

Next place on each side the *Lady Cullum*, a variegated Geranium, and the *United Italy*, with its leaves edged with silver. Both of these plants give scarlet flowers, but as they are grown principally for their leaves, you will nip off all buds. *Bouvardia Elegans*, with its coral, trumpet-shaped flowers, should come next; on the other side, a pink *Monthly Carnation*, with its rich spicy bloom.

If the proportions of the box will admit, we would also plant *Tom Thumb Geraniums*, white and scarlet. Then at the four corners, add in the corners some of the different varieties of the *Chinese Primroses*, which bloom almost ceaselessly, sometimes eleven months in the twelve; then bring in an Alternanthera, with its brightly veined lance-shaped leaves, and a variegated *Sweet Alyssum* with its white cluster of minute flowers. Bulbs of the *Duc Van Thol Tulips*, or Crocuses or Hyacinths, may be added, taking care to sprinkle the holes made for their reception with sand, and to cover them with it. Shroud them in fresh green moss, so that the leaf buds may not start before they have taken deep root, which will enable them to support and nourish the gorgeous flowers which lie embedded in their bosoms. Thus shaded, all will grow, and soon delight you with their fragrance.

One great advantage of these window boxes consists in the ease with which they are watered and cared for; there is no shifting of pots, or other manipulations. With a good moist temperature, and protection from frost at night, these box gardens will be a constant succession of bloom from early winter to leafy spring

If proper fastenings are provided, these boxes may be placed out doors, just on the window sill, or may have temporary staging erected for the purpose, and there be tended and sprinkled without fear of damage to either window or furniture. Here, in the open air and balmy days of spring and summer, can be grown Verbenas, Heliotropes, Fever Fews, Geraniums and trailing vines, like *Tradescantia, Moneywort*, &c., and there will always be flowers for a bouquet or a button-hole.

In an eastern or north-eastern window, *Fuchsias, Mignonette and Pansies*, which shun the heat, can be grown to advantage.

Plant Stands.

Here again we meet with an endless variety of designs and forms of construction. Every conceivable form of taste, has been devised and executed, and we are at no lack of convenience, but rather in a quandary, what to chose from so many things that are so good.

Fig. 47.—Design for Plant Stand.

Fig. 49 is a very pretty little flower basket, made of wire work, painted green. It is supported underneath by a frame work of wood, either oak or pine, neatly decorated, and having castors attached by the legs, for ready removal.

A zinc tray of perhaps four inches depth, is fitted inside the wire, which holds all the earth and water, (which all other baskets of this construction should have.) A small aperture for the withdrawal of the water, is fitted with a small stop cock, which should be hidden from sight. The plants kept in here, are to be packed in moss and will, with occasional watering, keep fresh and green upon the surface.

Fig. 48.

Figs. 50 and 51 are simple stands to be used for the same purpose, or can be adapted to the keeping of cut flowers. The top of No. 51, is covered with a small movable brass wire grating, the meshes being half an inch square, to support the flowers, and keep them in an upright position.

Fig. 50 is more convenient for preserving small plants, just in bloom, packed in with moss. This is, also, covered with wire work of brass.

Fig. 52 is a plant table, made of any style of wood, the heavier the better. It is of considerable depth, and will hold a large quantity of earth, is also lined with zinc or copper, and provided with a waste pipe. Around the top is a basket work of brass, usually four to six inches in depth. The pots placed inside are supposed to be deep enough to reach only to the lower edge of the brass work, and covered with moss. Cut flowers, Dahlias, Pinks and Carnations, may be placed in here, half of the box having previously been filled with moss, and

Fig. 49.

Fig. 50.

the rest with sand, into which their stems are pressed. If the flowers are tastefully arranged according to harmony of colors, they will give a pretty effect, and the flowers will last several days.

If it is possible, it will be well to provide all stands used for cut flowers, with glass shades which can be removed during the day time, but at nightfall be placed over them, both to secure from too cool temperature, and to protect against dust which comes from the morning's sweepings. Flowers will also keep fresh longer if preserved in moistened sand, than if kept in water alone.

Fig. 51.

Fig. 52.

Fig. 48 is a plant stand for household use and ornament of more than customary spaciousness. It is constructed either in a full circular form or semi-circle to suit the fancy, and will usually fit into the recess of any bow-window. It is built of a wire frame, principally with wooden legs and supports. Has the usual zinc tray inside, well filled with growing plants. Its size is about four and a

WINDOW GARDENING

Fig. 53.

Fig. 54.

Fig. 55.

Fig. 56.

Fig. 57

half feet in diameter, and stands two and a half feet from the floor. The illustration represents a [ ]t variety of plants within, fully 50 varieties, from Roses

Fig. 58.   Fig. 59.

Fig. 60.   Fig. 61.

and Fuchsias, to Ferns, Coleus, Bulbs and Primulas It is a happy gathering of floral treasures.

WINDOW GARDENING 73

Figs. 60 and 61 are two exquisite flower stands, very suitable for setting in the parlor window, just under the drooping lace curtains.

Fig. 62.

Fig. 61 is constructed of iron, but has a basin above filled with sand, in which may be grown either bulb or cut flowers, placed in moist sand.

Fig. 60 is a lovely basket of rustic work, principally of the same material as that from which our cane chairs are constructed. It is filled with ferns, drooping plants, Smilax, and has a great variety of other plants too numerous to mention in detail. Such a basket can be easily obtained or constructed at any furniture store, and filled by any florist.

Fig. 62 is of Terra Cotta, delicately moulded in the form of a vase rather than a plant stand, and filled with a profusion of charming plants from Tulip to Achyranthus, and Snow Drop to Fuchsia.

Every one who wishes to learn the best plants for such purposes will find full descriptions in Part Two.

Figs. 53 to 59 need little explanation. Every one has necessity for some plant stands for the pots before the window. All these designs are constructed of iron or made of wire and in countless patterns and devices. The cost is but very moderate, ranging from $5.00 to $25.00. All are easily movable and light.

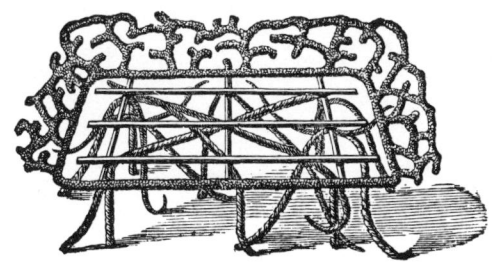

Fig. 63.

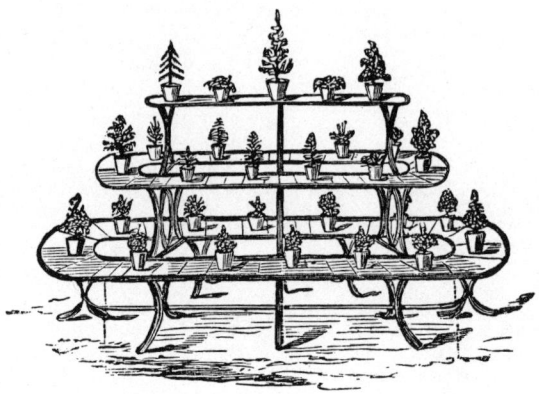

Fig. 64.

WINDOW GARDENING. 75

Ornamental Parlor Stand

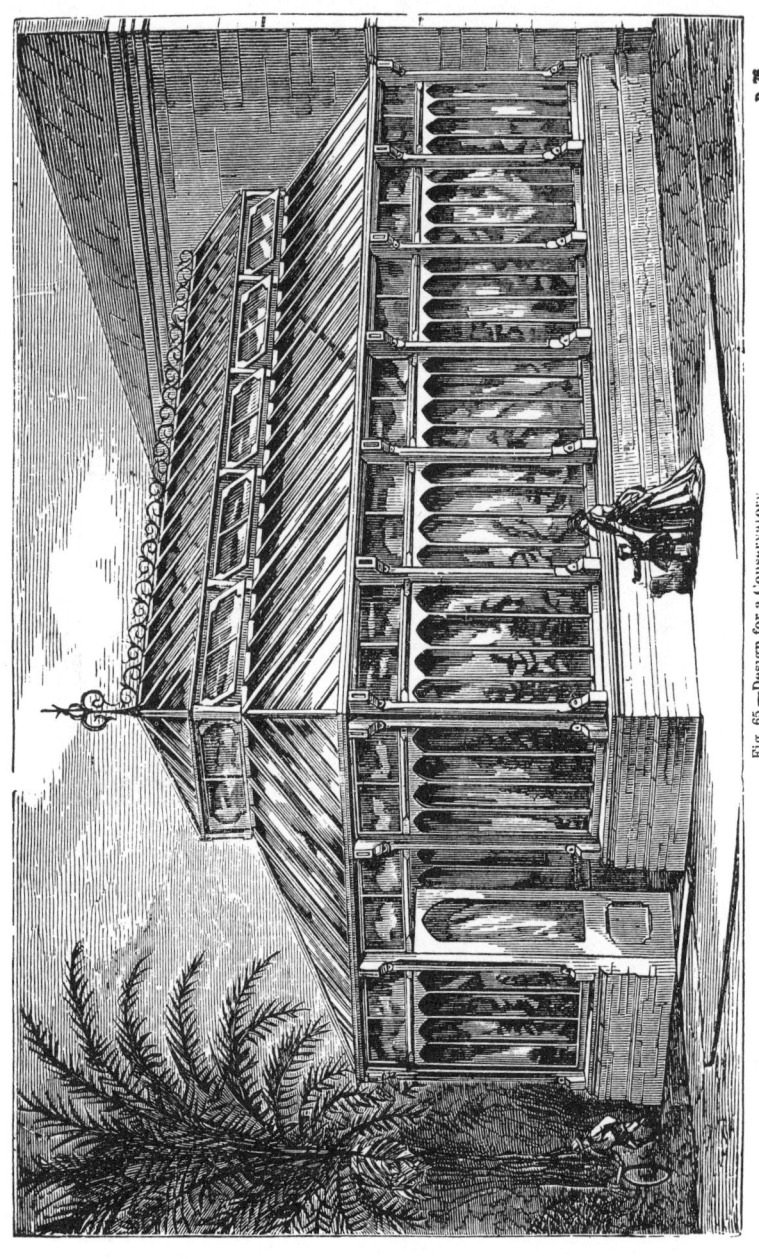

Fig. 65.—Design for a Conservatory.

CHAPTER IX.

CONSERVATORIES AND GREENHOUSES.

These are costly and mainly afforded only by the wealthy. As an ornament of architectural value, no villa is complete without them, and even the owner of the city mansion does not seem well satisfied till he has added one of these elegancies to assist the look and feeling of taste.

Usually they are quite costly, and both interior and exterior are highly decorated, and as objects of effect on the lawn, or among the shrubbery, they are worth all their value in their embellishment of rural art.

Still, even the person of moderate purse, may have one not very showy, yet very convenient, and well adapted to this purpose, viz: The keeping of plants in larger quantities than the ordinary space of the window, or parlor garden, and also in a better and more successful atmosphere than that of the living room.

It would take a volume alone to point out all technical details necessary to any one about to build one. For an extensive design, the advice of a horticultural architect is indispensable, but for home purposes, a design such as any carpenter can erect is seen in one of our succeeding plans.

Conservatories and green-houses are also somewhat distinct in their uses. The one is mainly devoted to ornamental purposes, and the exhibition of plants in full beauty of growth and bloom, while in the humbler green-house, propagating boxes are the chief furniture used by the gardener, for the production and forcing of his young plants. Still either term is appropriate, and the term greenhouse includes both.

Costly conservatories are built of iron and glass, more moderate ones of wood and glass. In building them, due heed must be given to ventilation. If in small home conservatories, they are not well heated, it would be well to have heavy out side shutters, so as to be rolled down at night, or double window panes of glass · usually a flue from the furnace which warms the house will, in most latitudes, give sufficient warmth, provided the furnace will keep up a uniform degree all night. This, after all, is not regular in large conservatories; and then the only satisfactory mode of heating is by pipes of hot water from a furnace specially constructed for the purpose.

If there is danger of frost, and it is feared that the heating arrangements are not sufficient, turn all the heat of the furnace into the conservatory. Yet there is on the other hand considerable trouble from having too much heat or light in the evening, especially if the conservatory is entered immediately from the drawing room.

Houses that are warmed by water pipes, branches of which are allowed to run through the conservatory, not only keep up a more steady heat, but afford considerable moisture to the atmosphere, and are of decided advantage.

Every Autumn, apply a coat of paint, not only to render it fresh and clear, but to fill up all hiding places for insects, and clear them out if perchance they have obtained possession, and in September early, put the pots and plants in their proper places. It is not desirable that they should remain out later than that.

Fig. 66.   Fig. 67.   Fig. 68.   Fig. 69.

For hanging pots up against the side of the house or wall, the *floreteen* is a convenient little utensil, constructed of a double iron hoop, bent in the middle at an angle of 90° and reversible. Cost is very trifling and made by any blacksmith.

When filling your house with plants, clean the pots well, and turn out the balls of earth to see that the roots have sufficient room, and are in a healthy state.

It is well, also, to scrape away the surface soil, and supply fresh compost.

Give your plants plenty of room, not crowding too thickly, allowing free circulation of the air, for then it is easier to keep them perfectly clean and healthy

Heliotropes, Verbenas, Geraniums, and indeed all herbaceous plants should be placed as near the glass as possible, as they require much sunlight, while variegated leaved plants Mignionette, Camellias, Primulas, &c., will not flourish luxuriantly, if the hot sun shines on them at noon day.

Fig. 70 is a design of a small home conservatory attached to the side of a village residence and entered from the parlor. Its length is about eighteen feet and width twelve to fifteen, affording all necessary room for a good home plant conservatory.

Such a house is heated either by a flue from the furnace, supposed to be placed in the basement of the house, or there may be a stove placed in depression of the floor at one end of the conservatory, and with pipes running from a drum lengthway each side to the other end, and returning to it again, may heat the room sufficiently; but there would be nothing to prevent a low temperature at night, unless some one could see that the fire was kept steadily burning. The most steady heat would come from the flue of the same furnace which heats the house. There are stands running around each side of the conservatory and a large square one in the middle.

The cost made by any carpenter, if constructed of wood, will be from $250 to $400, and if he has taste may be richly decorated and painted for that sum. A good conservatory could not well be built for a less price.

For a more elegant design still, we commend Fig. No. 65 of a beautiful form of architecture, lofty enough to admit of palms or tall ferns; large enough for abundance of fresh air, not close or stifling, and of a character highly ornamental for any situation. It is constructed of iron, yet nothing prevents it from being made of wood. The glass is in long lengths corresponding to the general style of construction. Ventilators in the top are easily opened or closed by pulleys.

Fig. 70.—A Village House with Small Conservatory.

There is a door for entering to the drawing room, also, one opening upon the lawn, with ornamental flower beds laid out along its side; it forms a design of rare and pleasing taste.

For out door plant houses separated from the dwelling we show designs of two styles.

Fig. 73 is still more artistic than the other, elevated upon a parterre embankment and surrounded with evidences of garden embellishments. This, also, is of iron, still it may be constructed of wood; is about twenty feet wide and from forty to fifty feet long; cost not less than $5,000. Most of the green houses in this country are now built upon the plan of low curved roofs, which afford great economy of space and heat, yet we believe variety and taste will admit the use of other styles. Such a one as this is a novelty in this country

Fig. 71.—Interior of the Government Conservatory at Washington, D. C.

Rarely have we seen any thing like it, presenting as it does a decided look or richness and elegance in the rural grounds of any wealthy villa proprietor. It is worth adoption.

Fig. 72 is intended purely for ornamental purposes suitable for the grounds of those of humbler means than they who can afford such rich designs as our last. It is a straight roofed span conservatory with cast iron fronts; sides about four feet six inches high with top and bottom ventilation, glazed with twenty-six ounce sheet glass, enamel painted throughout with ornamental finish, crestings, &c. This style of conservatory is set upon a foundation of white stone or granite, which gives a fine contrast with the green and shrubbery

In general the handsomest, lightest, strongest and most serviceable conservatories are constructed of iron frames, yet few or none are made in this country and no one offers them as a specialty. We find nearly all the best styles and designs of this character offered only by English horticultural manufacturers.

In England, nearly every one has either its Window Garden or its green house, and scarcely any family of intelligence but knows something of culture and propagation of indoor plants.

Fig. 72.—A Small Greenhouse.

Here we love these delicate treasures dearly and our taste is rapidly developing in this branch of rural pleasures, yet the green house is still to many a mystery, and seems an enormous expense. If good and suitable designs could be built for $100 to $500, their number would be quadrupled every year, and their general use be considered a desirable fashion.

An important consideration in the management of greenhouses is an abundance of light. It is quite essential that the conservatory should be placed on the sunny side of the house, and that its windows or door should open into the parlor or dining-room, and, if possible, avoid planting trees too near to cover it with their shade. If the location is southwestern or northerly, much more heat will be required; and both for economy and enjoyment, only one position is desirable, and that is southerly.

Fig. 73.—An Ornamental Lawn Conservatory.

Ventilation should be arranged so that the air will circulate *over* the tops of plants, and not upon the surface of the pots.

The slope of the roof should be at an angle of 45°, as this has been proved to afford the greatest amount of heat from the sun's rays.

A low staging upon which the pots are to be placed, should run all around the conservatory, and if it joins the wall, climbing vines may be planted which will clamber over it, or brackets may be put up, which will hold pots of drooping plants. If tastefully constructed, the floor should be made of tiles with pretty patterns, and even various plant boxes may be made of them.

The plants would flourish better if they were sunk in beds of sand, mould or moss, instead of separate pots upon a staging.

A thermometer is needed in every green-house, in order to regulate the temperature, and it should hang where it cannot be affected by the rays of the sun. The temperature should not exceed 66° by day, nor fall below 45° at night.

Watering.—Water the plants as soon as the ball of roots begins to dry. This will be visible on the surface, or by knocking against the pot. If a full, deep sound is heard, there is sufficient water; if a clear, hollow sound, water is needed. All plants of a rapid growth, luxuriant leaves, and masses of flowers, require more watering than others of a delicate habit. Ferns and tropical plants must have plenty of water; succulent plants require less water.

Watering may be done by a sprinkler or syringe, and care must be taken to give water to the soil and roots, as well as to the leaves, which, if watered from overhead, may often shed it and prevent any from reaching the pots.

Apply the water either at night, or so early in the morning that the heat of the sun will not injure the plants. Let the water stand or drip awhile before wiping up, permitting the moisture to permeate the atmosphere; after two or three hours the remaining water can be cleared away.

Steps or a ladder are necessary also, to use in removing plants from the staging, and also to assist in watering. Standing upon them a person with a watering pot can produce a miniature rain, which will tend to keep away all insects, and also wash the leaves effectually.

Once a week give in your waterings a stimulant such as has been mentioned in previous chapters

The plants should also be frequently turned around so as to keep them in good shape, and by frequent changing of position all have a chance at the best places.

All the directions minutely given in former chapters as to culture, propagation, potting, repotting, will apply as well to conservatories as to ordinary window gardening.

Plants.

For the greater convenience and accommodation of private citizens, lovers of plants, or, perhaps, not well instructed gardeners, we give a list of decorative plants for greenhouses and conservatories, which are distinguished by masses of flowers, fine leaves, interesting habits, and easy cultivation. We do not use for

WINDOW GARDENING.

this list any catalogues of nurserymen, nor do we make a collection from books or advertisements. We have carefully selected only such plants as are recommended by long experience in cultivating plants, and thorough botanical knowledge. Every plant which this list contains is for sale in this country.

Avoid an unfit composition of every possible or heterogeneous plants; the effect will be very poor. For instance, tropical plants do not mix well with plants taken from colder climates. Plants with expanded branches or like habits, are suitable mainly for standards, for vases, stands, etc.

Plants of a fine and graceful habit should have a free and light position. Put *Camellias, Azaleas, Rododendrons, Magnolia grandiflora, Viburnum tinus, Eugenia australis*, etc., as soon as they leave off blooming in the background, and move in the front row the following: *Acacias, Polygala, Metrosideros, Leptospermum, Franciscea, Melaleuca, Edwardsia microphylla, Diosma, and Erica.*

For *groups of plants* which have a *tropical character*, place so that they may show well: *Begonia, Ferns, Lycopodia, Amaryllis, Eucharis, Peperomias*, besides all plants with variegated leaves or thick foliage. For the background may be mentioned: *Ficus elastica, Cooperi australis, Gardenia; Fortuni, Musa, Heliconia, Bambusa, Eugenia Iambos, Justicia carnea, cristata, Porteana, speciosa*, etc. He who prefers succulent plants, and intends to keep his greenhouse filled with them, will not have much difficulty in arranging them, as they can be easily put in little groups, according to size and habit.

I. LIST OF PLANTS FOR A SMALL CONSERVATORY, GREENHOUSE, OR FLOWER-PARLOR, which is frequently visited by the family or visitors. The temperature of the house is to be temperate at night; in the day time thermometer may go up a little higher, as this will be the case when the sun is out. The situation of the greenhouse may be in a southern, eastern, or western direction.

a. PLANTS FOR STANDARDS, CENTRE OF GROUPS, STANDS, COLUMNS, ETC.:

Araucaria excelsa, imbricata, Brasiliensis; Aralia leptophylla, Sieboldii papyrifera; Chamærops excelsa, humilis, tomentosa, and stauracantha.

Rhapis flabelliformis; Sabal minor, Seaforthia elegans, Chamædorea lunata, Schiedeana, gracilis, desmoncoides: Latania borbonica; Corypha australis: Dracæna draco, Brasiliensis, terminalis, ferrea, Cooperi, stricta, rubra, congesta, australis, indivisa, and *Veitchii; Yucca gloriosa, aloifolia fol. var, flaccida,* and *quadricolor; Uhdea pinnatifida, Senecio Giesbrechtii, Melianthus major; Solanum Warscewitzii; Alocasia cucullata, odorata,* (*arborea,*) *macrorrhiza fol. var Caladium cupreum,* (*porphyroneurum,*) *pictum.*

b. PLANTS FOR DECORATION IN GENERAL:

Azalea indica, best new varieties; *Camelias*, best imbricate varieties; *Rhododendra, arborea,* and *hybrida; Acalypha tricolor; Andromeda floribunda: Trimalium fragrans; Leucopogon Cunninghami; Allamanda neriifolia; Aphelandra aurantiaca, pulcherrima carnea, superba, Porteana cristata, Leopoldii; Justicia speciosa; Ruellia varians; Eranthemum pulchellum, Cooperi, tubercu latum ; Ardisia crenulata, Brexia Madagascariensis , chrysophylla, serrata ; Brugmansia sanguinea, floribunda; Comaclinium ianthinum; Croton pictum, variegatum; Cyperus alternifolius! Panicum plicatum, fol. var.; Curculigo recurvata; Aspidistra lurida, fol. var. (Plectogynæ); Eucharis candida; Varlota purpurea; Amaryllis vittata varietas; Ficus elastica, Cooperi and australis; Franciscea latifolia, exima, hydrangæformis; Maranta sanguinea, zebrina, vittata; Gardenia citriodora, radicans, Fortuni and florida grandiflora; Mahernia odorata; Hibiscus rosa Sinensis var.*, double kinds, *Cooperi, splendens; Inga pulcherrima; Edwardsia microphylla; Jasminum Sambac, Duchesse d' Orleans, gracile; Lasiandra, splendens, macrantha; Psidium Cattleyanum; Magnolia fuscata; Olea fragrans, ilicifolia; Myoporum parvifolium, crystallinum; Eriostemon buxifolius, scabrum, neriifolium, intermedium; Medinilla magnifica; Meyenia erecta; Plumbago cærulea; Calla Æthiopica minor ; Tecoma Capensis ; Solanum capsicum, fol.* var.; *Vinca rosea* and *rosea alba; Abutilon Thompsonii, venosum floribundum, vexillarum, fol. var.; Acacia armata, paradoxa, dealbata, lophanta, pulchella magna, floribunda, melanoxylon, glaucescens, mollisssima, lineata verticillata, vestita; Agapanthus umbellatus; Bambusa Fortunei var ; Bouvardia leiantha, splendens, jasminoides; Cassia floribunda; Centaurea candidissima, plumosa, gymnocarpa; Cestrum aurantiacum; Iochroma tubulosa, Warcsewitzii; Linum trigynum; Chorozema ilicifolia, varia; Citrus sinensis, myrtifolius, aurantium, nobilis* (Mandarin); *Clethra arborea; Sparmannia Africana; Clivia nobilis; Cyclamen persicum, Coum, repandum; Cytisus Atleyamus, racemosus; Genista canariensis; Daphne indica rubra; Diosma alba, ambigua, ciliata; Echeveria secunda glauca, metallica grandiflora, sanguinea, racemosa, gibbiflora; Cotyledon cristatum, orbicu lare, rhomboideum: Crassula coccinea,* var. kinds; *Rochea falcata; Sempervivum arboreum fol. var., tabulæforme, canariense, orbicum; Sedum fabaria, telephium fol. var. Sieboldii variegata, dasyphyllum; Mesembryanthemum spectabile, coccineum, aureum, deltoideum, echinatum; Kleinia repens, ficoidea; Eugenia australis; Habrothamnus elegans, fascicularis ; Indigofera australis, decora; Laurus Camphora: Melaleuca alba, hypericifolia, decussata, ericæfolia, foliosa, lucidula, squarrosa, thymifolia, ovata, linearifolia, speciosa; Phormium tenax; Pittosporum Tobira; Polygala Dalmaysiana, grandis, speciosa; Rhododendron Gibsonii, jasminiflorum, Princess Royale, Veitchianum; Rhopala corcovadensis, Schizostylis coccinea; Statice arborea, Halfordii, macrophylla; Veronica Andersoni, imperialis, salicifolia, speciosa floribunda; Libonia floribunda, Centradenia floribunda, grandifolia ; Clerodendron infortunatum, fallax, Balfouri, Kaempferi; Coleus,* var. kinds; *Heliotropium,* var kinds ; *Poinsettia pulcherrima; Nandina domestica; Rogiera cordata; Rondeletia speciosa; Russelia juncea; Sanchezia nobilis; Scutellaria mociniana; Solandra grandiflora; Aloe fimbriata, Tabernæmontana coronaria fl. pl., Crowea saligna; Diplacus puniceus floribundus ; Farfugium grande; Ligularia Kaempferi fol. var. ; Callistemon semperflorens; Begonia ricinifolia, ricinifolia maculata, heracleifolia, macrophylla, Huegelii, Hernan diæfolia, grandis, Dregei, peltata, Pearcei, manicata, hydrocotyledes,Warszewitzii, coccinea, sanguinea, incarnata, odorata, argyr tigma, stigmosa, smaragdina, Rex* var. *hybrides, Sedenii, Weltoniensis,Boliviensis.*

c. PLANTS FOR HANGING BASKETS, FLOWER STANDS, LAMPS AND CANSOLES, ETC.:

Leucophyta Brownii, Vinca major fol. var.; *Mesembryanthemum cordifolium fol.* var.; *Crassula spathulata; Sedum carneum variegatum; Cerastium tomentosum, Biebersteinii; Tropæolum majus fl. pl.; Clematis azurea grandiflora, lanuginosa, Jackmanni; Ficus stipularis* (repens); *Gelsemium nitidum; Æschinanthus zebrinus, grandiflorus; Tradescantia zebrina, Warscewitzii; Saxifraga sarmentosa, Sieboldii fol.* var.; *Clorophyton Sternbergianum; Lonicera brachipoda aureo-reticulata; Solanum jasminoides; Isolepis elegans; Fragaria indica; Euonymus radicans; Ajuga reptans fol.* var.; *Glechoma hederacea fol.* var.; and var. species of *Selaginella.*

d. PLANTS FOR FESTOONS, COLUMNS, AND FOR DECORATING WALLS, ETC.

Passiflora actinea, cærulea, racemosa, edulis, insignis, quadrangularis, kermesina, Loudoni, trifasciata, princeps; Tacsonia splendens, Van Volxemii; Rhynchospermum jasminoides, obtusifolium variegatum; Cobæa scandens fol. var; *Akebia quinata; Stephanotis floribunda; Pilogyne suavis; Bignonia venusta, speciosa, australis, Latrobea; Tecoma jasminoides rosea; Mandevillea suaveolens; Phaseolus Caracalla; Physianthus albens; Thunbergia laurifolia, gran. diflora; Mikania scandens (Senecio micanoides); Tropæolum pentaphyllum, tricolorum, speciosum; Pharbitis Learii, ficifolia, insignis, palmata; Maurandia; Lophospermum; Rhodochyton volubile.*

e. FERNS FOR GENERAL DECORATION WHICH REQUIRE A MODERATE TEMPERATURE:

Acrostichum alcicorne (Platycerum); Adiantum tenerum, concinnum, cuneatum, formosum, pubescens, trapeziforme; Anemia villosa; Aspidium molle, violascens, Kaulfussia; Asplenium flabellifolium, palmatum; Blechnum australe, Brasiliense; Cyathea medullaris, australis; Cyrtomium falcatum; Davallia Canariensis; pixidata; Dicksonia australis, antarctica, umbrosa; Doodia caudata; Doryopteris palmata; Polypodium aureum; Gymnogramma chrysophylla, Peruviana; Lastræa elegans; Lomaria gibba, latifolia; Nephrolepis exaltata, tuberosa; Oleandra neriifolia; Pteris, longifolia, serrulata stricta.

II.—PLANTS FOR GREENHOUSES, CONSERVATORIES AND FLOWER SALOONS, WHICH REQUIRE DURING THE WINTER ONLY A LOW TEMPERATURE, OR HAVE A NORTHERN EXPOSURE:

a. PLANTS FOR THE GENERAL DECORATION.

Rhododendron hybridum, var. kinds; *Azalea Indica,* var. kinds; *Azalea amoena; Kalmia latifolia; Photinia serrulata; Aucuba Japonica,* new var.;

WINDOW GARDENING. 87

Ilex aquifolium, fol. var.; *Mespilus pyracantha*; *Eucalyptus*, var. kinds; *Andromeda floribunda*; *Kassandra canaliculata, speciosa, pulverulenta*, etc.; *Erica arborea, Mediterranea, hibernica, strigosa, herbacea, multiflora*; *Cryptomeria Japonica, elegans, araucaroides*; *Cedrus argentea (Africana)*; *Cupressus sempervirens, funebris*; *(Thuja) Biota filiformis*; *Retinospora*, var. kinds; *Fagus antarctica, Cunninghami*; *Laurus regalis, nobilis*; *Nerium oleander*; *Olea Europæa*; *Viburnum tinus, macrocephalum, suspensus*; *Magnolia grandiflora*; *Bambusa Metake, falcata*; *Polygala chamæbuxis*; *Rhuscus androgynus, racemosus, hypoglossum, hypophyllum, aculeatus*; *Abelia floribunda*; *Arbutus unedo, andrachne*; *Podocarpus elongatus, neriifolius, latifolius, elegans*; *Berberis Darwinii, dealbata, Fortunei, ilicifolia, macrophylla, Japonica*: *Buddlea globosa*; *Ceanothus azureus*; *Melia Azedarach, Pistacia lentiscus*; *Vitex agnus-castus*; *Cerasus lauro cerasus*; *Ceratonia siliqua*; *Cistus roseus*; *formosus, ladaniferus, Lusitanicus, grandiflorus*; *Leicesteria formosa*; *Coronilla glauca, fol. var*; *Daphne Fortunei, laureola, alpina, collina, cneorum*; *Elæagnus reflexa*; *Escallonia floribunda, grandiflora*; *Eurya Japonica, fol var.*; *Skimmia Japonica*; *Ophiopogon Japonicus, spicatum, Jaburan*; *Euonymus Japonicus, fol. var.*; *Juniperus Bermudiana*; *Rhamnus alaternus, fol. var.*; *Phormium tenax*; *Genista tinctoria, fl. pl.*; *Helianthemum*, var. kinds; *Hypericum calycinum*; *Jasminum revolutum, lucidum, Wallichianum*; *Ligustrum lucidum, fol. var., Japonicum, fol. var.*; *Mahonia Japonica*; *Myrica Californica*; *Osmanthus fimbriatus*; *Ulex Europæa*; *Yucca* and *Agave*, var. kinds; *Pinus lanceolatus*; *Pernettya floribunda*; *Stuartia pentagyna*; *Libocedrus Chilensse, nuciferus, Californicus*; *Magnolia conspicua.*

b. The following Plants may serve for heightening the effect of Flowers in the Winter-time and Spring:

Polygonatum stellatum, verticillatum, multiflorum; *Doronicum Caucasicum*, *Adonis vernalis, Dicentra spectabilis, Corydalis aurea, nobilis*; *Lindelophia spectabilis*; *Omphalodes verna*; *Cyclamen Europæum*; *Anthericum Liliago*; *Dodecatheon Meadia, Jeffreyi*; *Dianthus*, var. kinds; *Nardosmia fragrans,* (*Tussilago*); *Funkia, fol. var.*; *Gentiana acaulis*; *Primula cortusoides*; *Helleborus niger, Hepatica triloba, angulosa*; *Iberis sempervirens*; *Iris*, var. kinds; *Hyacinths*; *Narcissus*; *Crocus*; *Tulips*; *Muscari*; *Galanthus*; *Colchicum*; *Leucojum vernum*; *Trillium grandiflorum*; *Orobus vernus*; *Pæonia tenuifolia*; *Pulmonaria Virginica, saccharata*; *Ramondia Pyrenaica*; *Erinus alpinus*; *Soldanella alpina, minima*; *Rhexia Virginica*; *Sanguinaria Canadensis*; *Saxifraga ligulata, Sibirica, crassifolia, cordifolia*; *Spigelia Marylandica*; *Primula acaulis, fl. pl.*; *Viola*, var. kinds; *Lychnis Haageana, Sieboldii.*

c. Climbing and Hanging Plants for a house with a low temperature:

Adlumia cirrhosa; *Tropæolum pentaphyllum*; *Akebia quinata*; Various kinds of *Clematis*; *Ampelopsis Veitchii*, *Bignonia capreolata*; *Hedera (Ivy)* var kinds ; *Lonicera Japonica, grata, semperflorens, brachypoda aureo-reticulata, Cissus antarctica ; Rubus rosæflorus, fl. pl. ; Rosa sempervivens, Banksia, Thea, Noisette, multiflora, Fortunei ; Gaultheria procumbens ; Vinca minor,* var. kinds ; *Phlox verna, repens, setacea, Lysimachia nummularia ; Linnea borealis.*

d. FERNS WHICH CAN HAVE A LOW TEMPERATURE :

Adiantum capillus Veneris, pedatum ; Asplenium fontanum, marinum, ruta- muraria, viride ; Athyrium filix-fœmina, flexuosum, laciniatum, plumosum ; Blechnum boreale (occidentale), spicant (Lomaria) ; Cystopteris bulbifera ; Ono- clea sensibilis ; Lastræa filix-mas, rigida, dilatata, Goldiana ; Lomaria Magel- lanica, alpina ; Osmunda regalis, cinnamomea ; Polypodium vulgare, alpestre ; Polystichium aculeatum, angulare, acrostichoides ; Scolopendrium officinarum (vulgare) ; Struthiopteris Germanica ; Cyrtomium falcatum.

e. Finally, we add a small list of *Orchids,* or *air-plants,* for amateurs, who may cultivate them in a green house or flower saloon of a moderate temperature. The following species are free bloomers, not very tender, and easily cultivated :

Dendrobium nobile ; Cattleya Mossiæ, labiata, Skinneri, guttata, Perrinii, Laelia majalis, autumnalis, superbiens ; Calanthe veratrifolia, vestita rosea; Cypripedium barbatum, insigne, venustum ; Epidendrum ciliare, fragrans ; Gongora maculata ; Maxillaria tenuifolia, Harrissoniæ, picta ; Oncidium pu- pilio, roseum, picturatum, ampliatum, flexuosum, luridum ; Odontoglossum grande, pulchellum, Uro-Skinneri, Insleayi ; Lycaste aromatica, Deppii, Skin- neri ; Stanhopea tigrina, saccata, oculata, guttulata, insignis ; Schomburgkia crispa ; Acineta Humboldtii, longiscarpa ; Zygopetalum Mackayi, crinitum , Phaius grandifolius (Bletia Tankervilliæ, Limodorum) ; Peristeria alata ; Mil- tonia candida ; Cœlogyne cristata, Trichopilia tortilis; Cymbidium aloifolium, ensifolium ; Bletia hyacinthina

PART II.

PLANTS FOR WINDOW GARDENS

Fig. 1.—Design for Ornamental Hanging Basket.

CHAPTER X.

Hanging Baskets.

Hanging Baskets form our simplest and also cheapest style of window ornament. They need very little care, their demands are not very exacting, and the chances of failure are very much less than plants of more sensitive nature, fit only for careful pot culture. The Hanging Basket is supposed to be a modern invention, or, at any rate, not very popularly used until late times; hence, it strikes us with feelings of curiosity to learn that, in the observance of the Jewish rural festivals hundreds of years ago, plants and cut flowers were tastefully arranged, placed in vases, and suspended from the branches forming the roof of the leaf-covered tabernacle. This was made of the branches of the oak, cedar, palm, and willow, so cut as to prevent them from withering for seven days, while the Passover was celebrated.

The directions for culture are very simple: Choose as pots or baskets clay bowls of porous ware, which may be set inside either a wire or wooden frame, or a glazed vessel. In non-porous pots or vessels, plants will not grow to perfection; there is usually no outlet or drainage for the surplus moisture to escape, and all side ventilation or aeration is cut off. Hence, the soil becomes sodden, and the roots are liable to decay. After you have provided your baskets, then fill the bottom to the depth of an inch or two with small bits of charcoal, for the triple purpose of drainage, purification, and as a fertilizer. Charcoal dust is also desirable to mix with the soil. A coarse sponge might be put in, if the vessel is deep, to drink up the surplus moisture, and yet keep the soil moist by giving it out again when dry. You do not need a very rich soil; good garden soil is well enough; because, if too rich, your plants will grow too rapidly for grace and beauty, and run too much to stem. Climbing or drooping vines may run as much as they please; the more freely the better, as it is the very thing desired; but standard plants in baskets must not be stimulated much; they would outgrow their space.

Sand is a needed ingredient; at least one third the soil should be composed of "*scouring sand.*" Mix it well with dark loam and leaf mould. The soil from around pine trees is most excellent for your baskets; in fact, there is none better.

If the baskets become very dry from the excessive heat of the sun, it is best to place them in a dish of water for half an hour. Thus treated, the roots suck up a copious supply, and need not receive any more for two or three days.

Plants do not thrive luxuriantly in baskets, year after year, with soil or position unchanged; hence, it is well to renew them every autumn, for healthier plants will be the result.

In the summer time, when the rooms are closed against sun and flies, there is not light enough to keep the plants healthy, and then they should be hung in the shade of the porch or piazza, or under the trees.

Hanging Baskets, provided with the charcoal and the sponge in the bottom, need not have a hole for drainage, for these will supply their place.

Plants of very watery tissues, usually grown in the neighborhood of ponds or woodland streams, will do best in soil transplanted from such location; but ordinary leaf mould will answer for almost everything.

It is a good plan to keep a good reserve supply of soil at hand in a heap, ready at any time you may desire to make a new basket, fill a new pot, or change the plants in either.

When you are potting the plants into any vessel, press the soil well down around the plants, and never use wet soil; let it be well dried and friable

Watering should be carefully administered, for few know what to give their plants, how to give, or when. An hour's neglect or forgetfulness may blight the entire beauty of your basket; or, again, an overflooding in a hot, dry room may cause them to mould.

Whenever they are watered the whole of the soil in the pot should be well wetted, and the frequency of watering depends upon the temperature of the air; the warmer the room the more frequently will they need it. Usually once a day, in the early morning or previous evening, is sufficient, if the thermometer measures 45° to 65°; if over that, and averaging 60° to 80°, twice a day, watering moderately, will be sufficient. In winter time do not apply cold water: either use it of same degree as that of the room, or bring your dish of water in the room and let it stand an hour or two before applying. More damage than a little is done by applying too cool water, giving the tender plant a severe chill. If the surface soil cakes any, break it up frequently, and keep a good watch for insects.

Construction

The devices for making hanging baskets are nearly endless. Our florists offer a great variety of patterns; our wire manufacturers offer some pretty designs, and our pottery and tile merchants have equally attractive models of elegance and beauty. Choose anything you like, only we recommend to you not to get them too small. We would select nothing less than eleven or twelve inches in diameter, and six inches deep. Let the soil be filled in even with the edge of the rim, and then rise toward the centre like a small mound. If there are but one or two large plants in the basket, cover the surface of the soil with moss, which will retain the moisture in the soil, needing watering only at occasional intervals; the moss from trees is not as desirable as that usually found growing

Fig. 2.—Trailing Morning Glory—Convolvulus Mauritanicus.

on the ground in some low, moist place, near a swamp. Pots of lava, or non porous material, without a hole at the bottom for drainage, must be used only for holding other and more porous pots inside, the insterstices being filled with moist moss Very pretty wire baskets are found at some of our stores; and these, being open, must be filled with moss first, and then a little soil in the centre, and the plants added afterwards

Fig. 3.

Large sea shells, (nautilus or conch,) will hold soil enough to support trailers, and are usually very tasteful window ornaments. One of the prettiest baskets ever seen was made from a singe sea shell, quite large. Holes were bored through the edge to fasten cords to hang it by; the interior of the shell was filled with light, rich soil, and *Lycopodiums* and *Lobelias* were planted in it. The rind of the gourd, and of the scallop squash, make elegant baskets for drooping plants. Cocoanut shells, whether in their natural state or embellished, with rustic work around, are acceptable.

Home-made baskets of wooden bowls, (such as we use in our kitchens,) are very common and desirable. Four or five holes should be bored with a gimblet in the bottom or the sides of the bowl. The best sizes are 12 to 16 inches in diameter, and if there are no rustic arm supports, there must be several holes bored around the ed e, in which to fasten the cords it is supported by—three are enough.

Fig. 4.

To ornament the outside of the bowl, choose the gray and white lichens of the woods, fasten them on with glue, or nail on with small brads. If the stiff mosses from the pine woods are used, they can be wet with water, which renders them pliable, and fastened on with thread copper wire, nailing nails on the inner edge of the bowl and at the bottom, around which to twist the wires. The contrast between the gray and white moss, and the rich emerald or brightly variegated vines, is very beautiful. Such a basket, if planted with nothing more than the *Tradescantia zebrina*, and the green leaved variety of the same plant, mingled with soft hanging grasses, or the bright green of the *Moneywort*, would be very pleasing. City residents, of course, will not desire to make their own baskets, but prefer to get them filled from the most convenient florist. We introduce several very pretty designs, which deserve to be copied.

Fig. 1, is a design for a hanging basket of more than usual elegance, and is a specimen out of many favorite styles prevalent among the well-to-do classes o. Berlin, Germany. The box is made of handsomely carved wood, the inside lined with zinc or clay; the basin is filled with earth, and in it are planted Begonias, Caladiums, Coleus, Geraniums, Ivy, Ornamental Grasses, Calla Lily, and quite a variety of other flowers. The size is about two feet wide by three and a half feet long. Worsted cords and tassels help out the richness of the frames, and the brilliant hues of the foliage of the plants within. Few or no hanging baskets we have seen can equal this for artistic taste.

Fig. 2, is an illustration of a large, deep basket, filled with a dense growth of the *Convolvulus Mauritanicus*. This is a highly ornamental plant, of drooping, half shrubby character, slender habit, with a profusion of elegant light blue blossoms, **upward** of an inch in width, forming an admirable plant for suspended vases or baskets. It continues long in bloom, and its porcelain blue blossoms are conspicuously beautiful.

Fig. 5.—Group of Ferns.

Fig. 3, is a picture of the Convolvulus drooping over the sides of a rustic carved hanging basket. The outside framework is wood, but contains a clay bowl sitting neatly within. The Convolvulus family afford many very desirable plants for baskets of this description. One lady cultivator goes so far as to say that the common Morning Glory is one of the most satisfactory plants she ever cultivated. "The vine, by house culture, becomes delicate in form, and is very thrifty. The flowers, a little smaller than the Convolvulus tri-color, appear every morning, and remain until nearly night. Seeds planted in early spring, say March, will flourish and bloom in less than six weeks." This family generally are free bloomers, very showy, and have exceedingly handsome flowers, with rich colors.

Fig. 4, is a sketch of a pretty wire basket, filled with Ivy and Ferns; branches of the partridge vine hang over the sides of the basket; the interior is filled with moss, and over them all peep out clusters of exquisite ferns. The stems of the Ivy and the partridge vine are all stuck into bottles filled with water, and hid away here and there in the moss. The ferns had all been gathered from the woods, and then pressed out smooth and clean, and arranged gracefully, their stems standing in the water of the bottles; the bottles are filled with water every two or three days. The Ivy has also grown from only two or three little slips stuck into the water, and has twined its arms around and above the cords of the basket, clear to the very top.

Fig. 5, is a group of Ferns of great variety, gathered into a wire basket of neat and simple design. In the centre of the group is one of the *Dracænas*, having leaves of a brilliantly shaded dark crimson—a class of plants always very handsome.

Fig. 6.—Flower Basket.

Springing out of this is the *Goniophlebium subauriculatum*, with its long primate pendulous fronds; the *Cheilanthes spectabilis*, which delights in moisture, warmth, and shade; other Ferns, such as the *Maiden's Hair*, (Adiantum,) usually of large growth. The *Athyrium*, and many of the *Spleenworts*, (Asplenium,) are introduced here to form one of the finest styles of natural Hanging Baskets we can suggest for imitation by our readers.

Fig. 6, introduces a style of basket very suitable for bulbs. It is made of wire, and the interior is lined with zinc. There is a small vessel beneath to hold drippings from the hole for drainage. Zinc vessels are not always permanent; in time they corrode, and must be renewed. Clay or wood are preferable. The plants herein are several Hyacinths, Tulips, Crocuses, Lily of the Valley, &c. The directions for the starting of these bulbs and their culture has already been explained in the chapter on bulbs.

Fig. 7.—Ornamental Hanging Baskets.

Fig. 8, is a Conservatory Basket, of lava ware, made unusually deep. The plants herein placed are Dracænas, Crotons, Indian Ferns, Niphobolus pertusus, and N. rupestris; also the Variegated Panicum. Ivy droops over the sides.

Fig. 9, is an ornamental hanging pot of lava or Majolica ware, covered with drooping vines. The most popular favorites for drooping vines are the Nasturtium, Tropæolum, Convolvulus minor, Honeysuckle, Trailing Mesembryanthemum. The centre may also be occupied with low growing plants, like the Verbena, Heliotrope, Petunias, Nemophilas, Lobelias, Mimulus, &c.

Fig. 10 is a sketch of the *Sedum Sieboldii*, a plant of very easy growth, and does best when kept in the greenhouse or conservatory. The soil most suitable is light, yet rich. Say turfy loam, 1 part; rotten dung, 1 part; sand, 1 part;

Fig. 8.

brick broken small, 1 part. It should be always under glass exposed to the full daylight, and have abundance of water. It is naturally a trailer, and will droop gracefully over the outsides of the pot, and will bloom most profusely. It should be watered carefully, so that no water will get on the leaves. Give it fresh air frequently. The habit of growth of the Sedum Sieboldii is very peculiar. From one central crown or stool appear a number of slender branches; at regular intervals come the leaves in groups of three, and these continue to lengthen until in the month of August, when flower buds appear at the terminals of each branch.

The average growth of good specimens is about one and a half feet long, and the flowers have a spread of nearly six inches. As described by Shirley Hibberd: "In every stage of growth the plant is a beautiful object, the leaves being

Fig. 9.

slightly concave on the upper surface, and covered with a delicate glaucous bloom. The flower-buds appear a long time in advance of the flowers, but when at last these open in September, their lively, rosy, pink hue and symmetrical disposition are remarkably beautiful, and contrast chastely and cheerfully with the peculiar tint of the leafage. After the blooms have faded the stems die down, and are immediately succeeded by a new growth from the root, and thus, if encouraged by good culture, a specimen will become larger and larger every year, and may ultimately be grown to colossal dimensions. It is one of the easiest plants to grow, and its habit is remarkably distinct and elegant."

Fig. 11 is a plant of the Variegated Ivy. This is both cheap, clean, needs little attention, grows rapidly, and is the most permanently attractive of all plants for the window. Were there no other plant than this in the window it might still be considered well furnished.

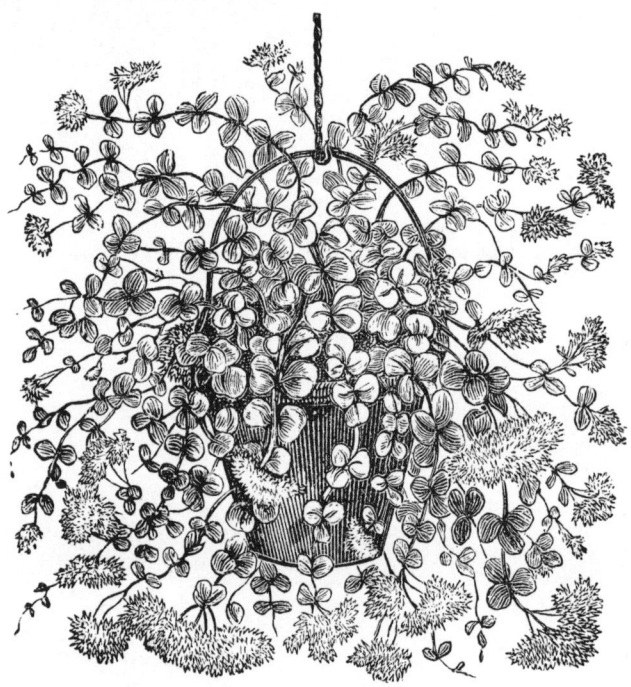

Fig. 10.—Sedum Sieboldii.

Fig. 12 is a sketch of the *Saxifraga Fortunei tricolor.*

Fig. 13 is a sketch of a bracket, with a wooden bowl, holding a plant of the Sedum Sieboldii trailing from it. This can be easily attached to the sides of the room, fastened to the centre of the window frame. It is very suitable for the Ivy either to trail from, or it may be placed at the bottom of the window, and the vine trained upward along the window casing.

Home-Made Hanging Baskets.

Nearly every one appreciates best some basket made by their own hands

WINDOW GARDENING

Usually only ordinary taste is requisite to contrive some very agreeable designs, and only a few hours' labor are needed. So we will give suggestions of how to make some Home-Made Hanging Baskets of handy and inexpensive materials.

For trimming the outside of some wooden bowl the roots of the laurel are very suitable, also those of the briar rose, which grows so plentifully near the woodlands and in fence corners. They are very crooked and gnarled, but when thoroughly cleansed from soil they can be nailed upon these bowls in grotesque and picturesque forms. A coat of copal varnish laid over the whole will often make the basket possess as handsome an appearance as those for sale by any florist.

Fig. 11.

The boughs and roots of the wild grape vine supply materials for this style of rustic ornamentation. Do not remove the bark unless it is very ragged, and then tear it away carefully, not taking more than is needful. By peeling in this way the stem will be vari-colored. If a darker hue than the natural wood is preferred, take two ounces of gum asphaltum and dissolve it in half a pint of turpentine or coal oil. Apply the stain with a common paint brush, putting on two coats if it is not dark enough at first.

A simple rustic basket may be made of three forked branches of any old tree, the more thickly bestudded with little branchlets, and the more gnarled and mossy, the better. Get those with drooping gray beard moss, if possible. The sticks should be less than an inch in diameter, and six or eight inches in length. Unite the three forks by their heads, winding them with very strong twine or pliable wire, and then, with the same material, fasten the branchlets here and there, to form a sort of lattice-work, and wind the gray moss over all fastenings. Then, in the same way, attach stout cord for handles. Set in this a common clay pot with its saucer, crowding around it plenty of moss, and you have a pretty thing complete.

Some persons take the common wire baskets, and make an improvement by surrounding them with strips of pasteboard. This is completely covered by pasting or glueing upon it gray or green lichens, with a few bits of the creeping moss, and a little of the coral or red cup moss. If none of this last can be procured, heat red sealing-wax, and with it touch the rough edges of some of the lichens.

Wire baskets are in general better suited for the conservatory than the par

Fig. 12.

lor, because they need a good watering two or three times a week, and will drip more or less constantly.

A very queer Hanging Basket was made by a flower-lover after this fashion: A piece of board one foot long and eight inches wide was first selected, then around the edges was nailed a lath projecting about an inch above; in each of the corners was driven a nail, and by means of strings tied thereto the basket was hung up. In the bottom were scattered a row of stones of moderate size; then they were covered with layer of earth; above this was another row of smaller stones, then a layer earth, then sand pebbles, and a final coating of earth over all, forming a mound in the centre. Here were planted very small rooted cuttings of trailing plants, such as the Morning Glory, which soon filled the basket to overflowing. Two plants only will be sufficient. The Cypress vine will be liked for the purpose. Choose five or six plants. The Madeira vine is unexcelled for such a position. Erect plants should not be chosen, although Verbenas, Abronias, and Thunbergias are not objectionable.

Where shells are used, they may be ornamented with different shades of moss, mixing the white mosses with the green as you glue them on.

The sections of large pine cones will also ornament prettily. Tack them on with brads, boring each scale with a brad-awl, so as not to split them. Alternate the scales, and varnish the whole, and you will be quite satisfied with the effect. It can be suspended with red or green curtain cord, fastened through holes, as before directed, with bows or rosettes at the top and sides. The cones of the dried burs of the Sweet Gum Tree, if strung together on wire or strong twine, as beads are arranged in fancy baskets, make a handsome basket, whose rustic appearance is very pleasing.

The simplest and prettiest of all these constructions is that made from small sticks of oak, maple, beach, or other wood, cut in lengths of eight, ten, twelve, or more inches, according to the size you desire. They must be about an inch in diameter, and a hole should be bored with a gimblet an inch from the end of each stick. They are put together in log-house fashion, one stick lopping over the other, and a wire with a loop on the upper end is passed through the holes at each corner, and bent up on the under side. A piece of board an inch thick is then fastened to the sides for a bottom, and the spaces between the sticks should be filled up with moss. Small iron chains suspend such baskets, and rich soil from the woods is the best to grow the plants that will twine round the chains and wreath them. Ribbons can be used if desired. We have seen more than fifty of these baskets suspended from the roof of an orchid-house, and the effect was exquisitely beautiful.

A cocoanut affords a very pretty miniature basket. Leave the husk on, and

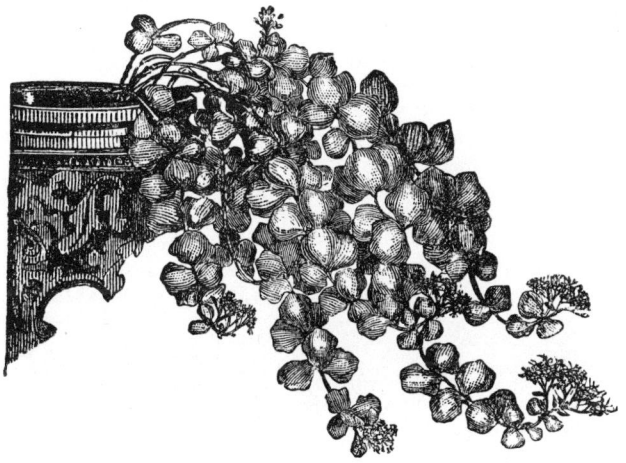

Fig. 13.

saw off about one-quarter of the nut; dig out the meat, and bore holes through three sides of it. The stem end is the part to be sawed off. Tie cords into the holes. There are many articles lying about every house that could do duty for hanging baskets. Worn out fly-covers can be lined with moss or cartridge paper, and when filled with soil and beautiful plants they produce as fine an effect as many a more picturesque affair. We saw one but recently covered with the golden flowers of the Moneywort, mingled with the bright blue of the Lobelia, and the Zebra-striped leaves of the Tradescantia, all growing luxuriantly, and making a humble cottage window a picture of grace and beauty.

Ox muzzles are within the reach of every country girl, and when painted green and lined with moss they form most desirable baskets to suspend from piazzas or trees. They will hang from the trees all winter, and in the spring th hardy vines, Moneywort and Partridge vine, (*Mitchella repens,*) come forth in fresh beauty and gracefulness.

Miniature baskets can be made of a goose or turkey's egg, that are exceedingly pretty and attractive. Select the largest size, make a hole with a needle at each end, and blow out the yolk and white. Then dip the egg into boiling water, and while it is hot cut it in the middle, a little at a time, for fear it will crack down too far. Use a pair of small, sharp sissors. For a covering and c rds to suspend it, take scarlet, green, or blue split zephyr worsted, and either net or crochet a cover. Use a fine mesh or needle, and make an ornamental scolloped edge around the top. Crochet cords, or twist them, of the zephyr, and hang the tiny baskets with them. Three baskets can be made and sewed together, with a cord attached to the edge of each shell. A different vine can be planted in each egg shell. Use a rich, but rather sandy soil, and the vines will grow luxuriantly.

The same device can be suspended from the chandelier to hold cut flowers, or the chains can be omitted and the baskets be used as vases

Boys or girls who possess any ingenuity can construct these pretty floral adornments in their leisure hours. Money is not always required for their manufacture, nor need those who live in the country apply to the florists for plants to fill them; for the fields and woods contain many twining vines that are very suitable for them. Almost anything will do for a basket—shells, horns, or anything that will hold earth, have been used for the purpose. Even turnips and carrots can be hollowed out and made to hold pretty little plants—so no one need be without these simple floral adornments for parlor or dining-room.

Plants for Hanging Baskets.

Our theme is now a more pleasing one, for how infinite, and yet indescribably beautiful, are some of the combinations of plants in baskets which we occasionally see.

Take, however, from us one general word of advice: Do not crowd in too many plants of upright growth. Usually one erect plant of showy, striking character, should be used—say a Begonia or a bright flowering Geranium; then around this gather your plants, of great variety, but lower and more compact growth, and around the edge plant both your climbers and your trailers. If your basket is to hang in a northern or eastern window, where the temperature is lower than any other exposure, you will have to choose such plants as the Lycopodiums, Periwinkle, and Moneywort. They will do well here, for they require less sunlight. An Ivy will do well anywhere, so you may consider this your safest plant. As we have mentioned before, it is not best to bring your plants immediately from the outdoors to the warm air of the living room. Do it gradually, by first bringing the basket, after it is filled, into a cool room with plenty of light, but not directly from the sun. Here let the plants get well started, and after two or three weeks you may bring the basket into the parlor or living room.

In making your choice of plants avoid the costliest favorites of the greenhouse; *i. e.*, it is better to take something which will thrive with ordinary culture. Greenhouse plants need more care than the window-gardener can usually give. A healthy flowering Geranium is more popular with nine out of ten than a Camellia, and is in proportion as much easier to grow.

A great trouble among amateurs is too great a fancy for seed-grown plants: *i. e.*, they purchase florists seeds, and aim to grow their own plants by sowing the seed in the basket. It is hardly necessary to say failure is the general rule, except in the case of a few climbing plants, which will grow well anywhere. If the amateur does not know enough about propagation to grow his own plants, it is much better to buy them already started from a good florist.

The list of plants may be arranged in several very distinct classes, as follows:

1. CLIMBING VINES—

The *Tropæolum Lobbianum*, flowers plentifully in winter, and its brilliant red flowers are very attractive.

The *Morning Glory* will grow readily in a sunny window, and its flowers are indeed a glory. A small vase can be used to plant the seeds, and it can be suspended with ribbons.

The vine of the *Sweet Potato* is very graceful. Quite a good many who have admired a basket covered with its leaves have felt a little chagrined to find it was nothing after all but a Sweet Potato vine. The tubers can be set into a glass small enough to keep the root three or four inches from the bottom. Fill the glass with water, and place it in a warm room; give it two or three hours of sunshine each day, and in two or three weeks it will begin to grow. All through the winter it will continue to develop its glossy green leaves in profusion. The *Discorea Batatas* is the best species for home culture.

Among other climbing plants are *Senecio scandens*, (German Ivy,) a very free grower; *Lonicera aurea reticulata*, with fine yellow variegated foliage.

There are no finer plants in general to be used than the Cobœas, Maurandias, Lophospermums, and Tropæolum. The Variegated Leaved Cobæa is a great favorite, either to dangle from a basket or clothe a trellis.

For Drooping or Trailing Plants the list is quite extensive. *Lysimachia,* or *Moneywort*—old, and hardly yet superseded.

Saxifragas,	Sedums,
Linarias,	Lobelia,
Yellow Flowering Gazanias,	Tradescantia,
Mimulus moschatus,	Nierembergia,
Mimulus tigrinoides,	Verbenas,
Ice Plant,	Mesembryanthemums,
The Partridge Vine,	Dew Plant.

The *Strawberry Vine* is a rapid runner, with leaves shaped like the strawberry but much smaller. Its flowers are white, and its seed-pods are formed of bright, cherry-red berries, which render the plant very ornamental.

The *Cranberry Vine* has been used for basket purposes with great success; its glossy, bright leaves, pure white flowers, and bright, coral-hued berries making it quite an acquisition to the list of trailing vines.

The *Coliseum Ivy* and *Smilax* are used perhaps more universally than any thing else. They are grown from seed readily.

The *Gazania splendens* makes a hanging basket exquisite in beauty; reaching down one to two feet from the basket, and blooming ten times better than it does in the open ground.

Among other good trailers are the Ivy-Leaved Geranium, Linaria cymbalaria, or common toadflax, Lysimachia, Nummularia Folea, the common Moneywort, single Petunias of free habit, Tradescantia bicolor, or zebrina, the purple and bronze leaves of which are admirable to mix with the trailing stems of *Vinca Elegantissima* and the variegated Ivies.

Of the Ivies, *Hedera latifolia maculata* is really superb if grown in a poor soil, in moderate shade, and abundantly supplied with water all the summer.

Mesembryanthemums do far better in hanging baskets than in pots, but are truly splendid plants when planted in a rich, sandy soil, with plenty of drainage, and fully exposed to the blaze of summer sunshine. A hot, sunny conservatory is a good place for them.

Mikania scandens will clothe a basket in a few weeks with its most elegant foliage of light green hue, and rich glistening surface. It should be moderately shaded, and kept in a cool atmosphere.

The *Polygonum suaves*, somewhat like the Dioscorea, is a free growing trailer of very neat habit, producing hundreds of little flowers, which emit a powerful perfume.

The *Sedum Sieboldii* is unsuitable in the open air. When placed in baskets and grown under glass, or in the conservatory, it will spread rapidly, bearing an abundance of its chocolate-colored flowers, while the glaucous hue of its succulent leaves presents a most striking appearance

Plants of Upright Growth.

Here you have a large list to choose from. Usually only one plant should be chosen if the basket is of moderate size. If the basket is very capacious, and you are bound to have a magnificent collection, you may combine all three classes, climbing or trailing plants, or those of upright standard growth.

You may select any of the numerous varieties of the Fuchsia, with their graceful, bending drops of bloom. *Petunias*, single or double. *Heliotrope*, always agreeable for their fragrance. *Carnations*, sweetly scented, blooming freely every month. The *Neapolitan Violet*, or the modest yet lovely little *Chinese Primrose*. The *Cyclamen Persicum*, with its curious flowers and valuable foliage, the popular Geranium. The *Daphne odorata*, which will fill your room with its sweet odor; or you may arrange around the edges of the vessel some Hyacinths, Crocuses or other bulbs. If you want plants of ornamental foliage, you will naturally turn to some of the numerous varieties of graceful Ferns or *Lycopodiums*. The Dragon plant *Dracœna terminalis*, has blood red foliage, and seems to be used more often than any other as a single plant. The *Begonias* and *Gesnerias* have rich velvety leaves. For curiosity you may want a *Cactus*, or a horseshoe *Geranium ;* for scent, the Lemon or Rose Geranium, or the well known scented Verbena, or the Musk plant. The little Cigar plant (*Cuphea*), is not very showy, but is esteemed for its constant blooming qualities.

Many use the Coleus and Achyranthes, when young, and possessing rich, delicate shades, they contrast well with their crimson or purple against the green of other plants, producing a good effect; but they soon grow too tall and look out of place. They can, however, be kept pinched back. This combination of color, either by contrast or harmony, is an excellent idea, and will not only give each plant an opportunity to display its peculiar habit of growth, but a novelty of color, likely to be appreciated by everyone.

Cissus discolor, leaves silvery white, shaded with purple.

Ficus repens.

Isolepis junciodes, ornamental grass.

Panicum variegatum, variegated grass, leaves green, striped with white and rose color.

Poa trivialis argenta, a new dwarf grass, variegated.

Tradescantia zebrina and *virides.*

Vinca elegantissima, variegata.

Selaginella variegata.

The *Ivy Leaved Geraniums* are very desirable, and L'Elegante with its light green leaves margined with white and pink, and its snowy white flowers, would be a gem for any window. This class of Geraniums are all of a low spreading or trailing habit, hanging down and flowering freely.

Myoporum parvifolium, a very neat trailer, bearing small white flowers in autumn, winter, or spring.

Monochaetum, is a beautiful winter flowering plant, but will require tying down at first, and then will trail nicely over the basket.

Ferns.—These form plants of permanent growth and habit, very suitable for hanging baskets. The soil needed for them to grow in, is equal parts of peat, loam, and sand, with some broken crockery mixed with it. One of the finest ferns for the basket is the *Polypodium vulgare,* or common *Polypody.* This may be grown, if desired, in nearly all moss, with the addition of only a very slight portion of soil.

The *Asplenium flaccidum,* is esteemed one of the handsomest, having a beautiful drooping habit, and yet producing little young ferns all over the old fronds. Place this in the centre of the basket, and display it so that its branches will show over the sides, with their bright lively green, and they will look extremely beautiful, fully justifying this as one of the best in cultivation.

Pteris serrulata, and *P. rotundifolia,* are easily grown, have a good habit, and prove to be very good Ferns for the basket.

The true *Maiden's Hair Fern*, (*Adiantum capillus Veneris*), by spreading at the roots will soon cover the surface of a basket.

The *Asplenium lanceolatun* and *A. marinum*, are also spreaders.

Ferns will always be beautiful plants for window culture on account of their delicate outline and tasteful droop of their branches. Every amateur, however, will do well to begin with two or three at first, and then study the rest gradually until he becomes familiar with their general characteristics. In watering Ferns, use warm water only, they will require it frequently also, for Ferns are natives of moist situations and latitudes; to most of them the dry air of a warm room is often injurious; closed cases are best.

The following trailing ferns are suited for hanging baskets: *Nothoclaena tenera, Davallia pentaphylla, Fadyema prolifera, Adiantum cordatum.*

The list of plants for baskets is endless; you are never at lack what to choose. You may begin with one plant, but as you become more acquainted with the nature of each plant, and learn their habits, you will love them so dearly as to sigh because you *have not room for more.*

How to arrange Plants in the Baskets.

We offer several plans of how to fill a number of baskets easily:

No. 1.—A fine low standard for a small hanging basket is the Primula Sinensis (Chinese Primrose), bearing white or crimson flowers. Soil—two parts garden mould and one part sand Water often, but slightly. Raise from seed or division of the root, in sandy soil. Take offsets from old roots in May, re-set them in fresh soil and keep the pots in the shade until September. Gloxinias—flowers of rose color or crimson—make a fine display in similar pots. They need the same soil as the Primula. Water scantily, except when in bloom. Propagate by division of the roots, or a single leaf set in damp sand. Just within the edge of the pot set Lysimachia nummularia (Moneywort), Nepeta glecoma (Ground Ivy or Gill run over the ground), or Coliseura vines. These have yellow, blue, white flowers. They will throw out trailers three or four feet long. Twine some of these around the chains or cords that sustain the basket.

No. 2.—In the same sort of pots and soil, with the same drooping plant, Cyclamen punctatum, or C Persicum—flowers white, pink or purplish—are very pretty. Or a root or offshoot of Mesembryanthemum crystallinum (Ice-plant), whose stems and leaves, when the sun shines upon them, glitter as if covered with pearls and diamonds. One of these plants will soon spread over the surface and hang prettily around the basket. The flowers are small—pale crimson or white. Or two or three Verbenas—white, scarlet and maroon, or white, pink, and purple—spreading and drooping, and creeping and climbing as they choose; they flourish much better thus than when trained and trimmed. Start new plants from seed, or small branches, every June. Keep them rather dry and shaded, till September, then give them plenty of sunshine and increase the water but never water them very freely

No 3.—In baskets of the same size—six inches; but in good garden soil only—set a Nierembergia gracilis, with its slender stems and fine foliage and pretty white or lilac flowers, together with a Mahernia odorata, of similar habits and foliage, with blossoms of pale yellow, very fragrant; and a Lobelia cœlestina, or L. gracilis, with its tiny leaves and delicate white or blue flowers, that will droop over the basket's rim. Start these plants and treat them like Verbenas, or Petunias of various shades, giving them the same treatment and allowing them to grow as they choose, like Verbenas. Or three or four bulbs of Oxalis, which, if started in August, after three months of complete rest in a dry state, will fill and cover the whole basket with their foliage and flowers from November till April or May. The varieties bearing white, scarlet and yellow, make a pretty group, or pink and white, and purple.

No. 4.—Baskets a foot in diameter, filled with the same soil, may hold a Zonale geranium—Tom Thumb, Fire King, or Mrs. Pollock; or Mountain of Snow, with its white-bordered leaves—and an Ivy-leaved geranium to climb up the handles; with a Maurandia, a Solanum, or two or three Vincas to trail around the brim and about the basket. Raise these all from branches rooted in sand under glass in May. Water frequently, but sparingly, till in bud, then give the fertilizer mentioned in a previous chapter, and plenty of water.

No. 5.—"A happy family," to fill a very large basket of good garden soil, should have one of the geraniums above mentioned for its centre; a Euphorbia, with silvery foliage; Coleus, maroon or bronze; a Bouvardia, scarlet flowers; a Sanguinaria, white flowers, and mignonette and alyssum, with moneywort, ground ivy, Irish ivy, Madeira vine, Solanum and Maurandia for climbers and trailers. Raise the standard plants from slips or branches rooted in wet sand, under glass, in May or June. Transfer them to the basket in September, and at the same time set with them cuttings of the vines. Keep the basket in the shade, and water it scantily for a month; then give it the full sunshine and water enough to keep the soil from crumbling. When buds appear on any of the plants, give it the fertilizer once a week for two months. Be sure that the air of the room in which it hangs is moist by the evaporation of water upon the stove or furnace, and open the window near by twice a week for a quarter of an hour, shielding the plants from the draught by newspapers pinned into cone shape around the basket. With this management the "happy family" will be your pride and delight.

Frame for an Ivied Garden or Conservatory Seat.

CHAPTER XI.

THE IVY FOR DECORATIVE PURPOSES.

The Ivy might be called the poor man's vine, for, like the Wilson Strawberry, it will grow for almost every one. It is the easiest of all the vines for indoor use, both in growing and for training, and not a little of its merits as a favorite window plant are its permanency, for it will live long in one pot without change of soil or position. It accommodates itself to all temperatures save that below freezing, and when in full growth it adds more grace to the window than any plant yet used.

The English Ivy (Hedera helix) is what is styled a *rooted climber*, as from every little joint roots will spring out and take hold of any support. This is one great advantage of value over other climbing vines which must be trained.

It is hardly adapted to our severe wintry climate, and will not live out of doors unless covered with straw. This renders its use for windows a necessity, and who that has ever gazed upon its glossy green leaves, drooping with long garlands of graceful verdure, but has felt it well deserved to be named the most beautiful of all drawing-room plant decorations. A writer speaks of the affection with which it is esteemed in German houses: "It becomes as one of the family. Sometimes the whole side of a parlor is covered with it, and twining around over picture frames, or looped about brackets, drooped over statuettes, the portraits of father, mother, and cherished friend, look forth smiling from the leafy environment. Small articles of *vertu* gleam here and there, touched with it, framed about mirrors or doors, each heart-shaped dark evergreen leaf, instinct with loveliness, adds to them all increased beauty. Wherever it goes it makes a green, perpetual summer of indoor life."

Another writer, viewing it in a poetic view, says: "A single root has been known to wreathe a bow window with thick garlands, and then strike off into lovely, independent paths along picture cords and above cornices, till the room seemed all a-bud, like Aaron's rod. It will cover a screen of wire, curtain a curtainless window, festoon a pillar, frame a favorite picture, (and what more graceful or delicate frame could be desired?) arch a door, climb and twist about a window-sill, and swing in long-looped tendrils from a bracket. There is no end to its beautiful uses.

"Tickle it with a little guano, and how it frolics. Nip off the terminal shoots, and lo, two bright, persistent tendrils shoot forth, and curl and twine about your very fingers. Wash its dusty leaves, and no child could look more gratefully in your face. It harbors no vermin, encourages no blight, but steadily and sweetly

112   WINDOW GARDENING.

keeps its daily course. It is a decorative artist of high ability; a companion, a friend."

Notwithstanding this poetic imagery, it must be admitted its presence, with

Fig. 14.—An Ivied Staircase.

its entwining, luxuriant foliage, gives a refreshing and pleasant look to every apartment; of uncounted worth is it in homes where garden facilities are few or none, and a sprig of green is considered equal to the nobleman's wide, rural estate

The Ivy requires rich soil in which to grow, and must have strong food.
"Of right choice food are its meals, I ween."
You must therefore select for it the best soil which your garden can afford; add to it one-half each of well-decayed manure and leaf mould rubbed together; then set the pan of compost in the oven and bake it, if you wish to kill all larvæ of worms and white ants.

Plant the roots in large, well-drained pots, with an inch or two of bits of charcoal at the bottom, and as the roots increase transfer them to larger-sized pots or buckets. The Ivy will grow in wood vessels as well as pottery, and pails or buckets painted green can be made to do duty for the pots.

Should the roots appear to be too thickly crowded in too small a pot, run a knife around the edge of the soil and turn over the ball of earth. If this is so, cut off a few of the outer ones, and then repot in rich soil in a little larger vessel.

The Ivy seems to be the least sensitive to changes of light of any plant we have; neither does it require much heat, thus being exceedingly well adapted to situations in halls or balconies, or rooms not very well heated. Figure 14 shows how it may be of great service in decorating a hall, the brackets holding the pots being fastened to the side of the wall, and the ivy permitted to climb up both wall and porch.

If planted in pots and trained to stakes, they can be readily moved from one window to another, or from one room to another; it is much the most convenient method to have the Ivy in some portable form.

Like all other plants, however, it must have a uniform temperature, and though it will bear a little chilling without much injury, yet it should be kept where there is some degree of warmth.

It delights in considerable moisture, and if neglected or permitted to dry up, its luxuriance soon suffers; hence, a saucer or pan should be kept full of water, ready at any time for its use.

During the spring and summer months the pots of Ivy are often carried to the outer air, and placed on the balcony or under a tree in the lawn or garden. Here they might be neglected; so we again repeat our caution: do not forget the water.

When brought into the house the leaves should be carefully washed with soap-suds and water; all unsightly branches and torn leaves removed.

Ivies for the house should be brought in before November, or even before it is time to build the fire. Place first in a cool room, and then bring gradually into the warmer room.

When placed where they are to stand, the vines should be gracefully arranged, and secured by small strings to the wood-work, or to the curtain by bits of green worsted braid. The green creeping foliage is a fine contrast to the whiteness of the delicate lace curtain.

Vines can be grown by immersing the stems in small vials of water, and fastening them to the backs of picture frames they are desired to ornament. With a number of vials quite a luxuriant growth can be imitated, but care must be had to keep the vials filled with water. At intervals, two or three bits of charcoal may be added to sweeten and purify.

Fig. 15.—An Ivied Picture Frame

A good illustration of how a picture frame may thus be decorated is afforded in figure 15, showing a looking-glass with rustic frame, and the Ivy twining around it. In this case no vials are used, but a very unique and convenient receptacle, shown in figure 16. Usually all our frames hang forward a little at the top from the wall, and leave an open space. This receptacle fits into this open space at the back of the top of the frame, and is very neatly concealed. To make this successful the frame should be of good size. The receptacle is wedge-shaped, and made of zinc by any tinsmith, and of the right length and diameter to fit in behind. After filling with earth plant the Ivy, and let its leaves ramble over and down the frame.

Such a frame should not be hung near a fireplace, for the heat and dust would hinder the growth of the plant very materially. If it can face a north or east window it is best situated. Water should be given daily at the same time the other plants usually receive this attention—by night or early morning. Note one thing, in filling this pan, to remember to place a few bits of crockery at the bottom, to secure efficient drainage. Avoid giving a surfeit of water,

A very novel style of ornament is afforded in Fig. 17, designed for a portable screen of Ivy. This is a box made very similar to those for the window, of a length varying from three to six feet, and one to two feet wide, mounted on castors. A number of laths of wood, neatly and smoothly planed, are nailed crossways, and fastened upright at the back of the box. Usually the height is about four to four and a half feet. The entire box and lattice-work should be painted green; then when dried fill the box

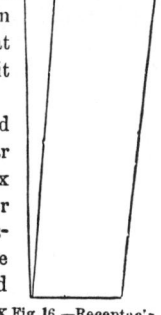

Fig. 16.—Receptacle for Ivy

with mould, and set in the Ivy plants, which, when well started, will soon cover the trellis completely

If desired, the front of the box may be ornamented by planting thickly Lily of the Valley or Primulas, or Mignionette, sown in the summer. Other climbing vines may be introduced either with the Ivy, or in place of it, such as the Morning Glory, Woodbine, Clematis. The box is an ornament in any position where placed, either before the window, or across the corner of the room, and the capacity of the box also affords opportunity for growing many choice standard parlor plants, Fuchsias, Geraniums, &c. Mr. Robinson states that such screens are used to a great extent in Parisian saloons and drawing-rooms, and in one instance saw them in quite a row, beautifully used to embellish crystal partitions between large apartments.

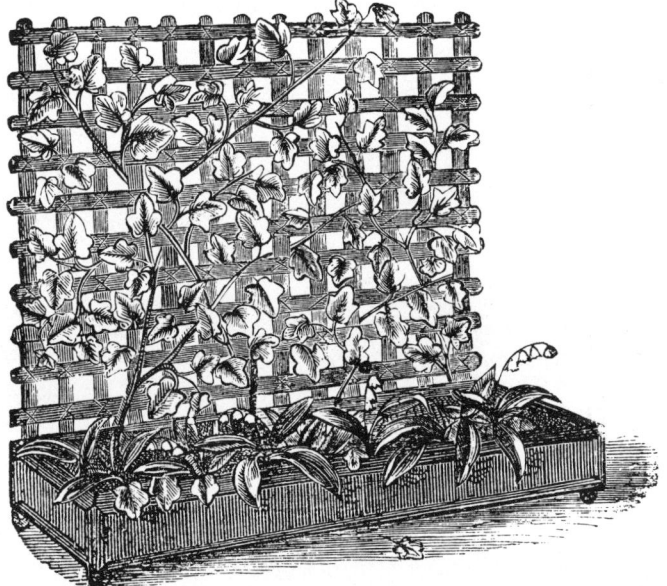

Fig. 17.—Ornamental Screen of Ivy.

One day in his rambles he came upon a wine shop in an obscure part of Paris, where the window was decorated with the Ivy; on going in, he found it planted in a rough box against the wall, up which it had crept, and was growing above as carelessly as if in a wood. At another time, at the Court of Versailles, in the porter's lodge, he witnessed the deep interest which the fat porter and his wife took in Cacti, &c., and their nice collection of other things, but more particularly at the sumptuous display of Ivy, which hung from over the mantelpiece. It was planted in a deep recess, and tumbled out its abundant tresses almost as if depending from a Kerry rock in its native home.

But its most successful use is in the hanging basket. Here at home it climbs, and swings, and droops at will, thriving and twining until the arms of the basket are hidden in the dense verdure. Probably no cheaper style of hanging baskets can be obtained than this, and surely none will last as long.

Another charming use to which the Ivy can be put is to twine it around an Easel in the parlor. Take a small rustic jardinet, such as are figured in one of the chapters of Part I, fill with earth, plant in it a good strong root of the Ivy, and then twine its long tendrils around the edges of the Easel, and let it droop from the top over the picture placed on the rest beneath. It forms one of the finest of draperies and borders for any art engraving, portrait or painting. Little brackets of it may be filled like Fig. 13, in chapter 10, and fastened in the centre of the side of any room, and while the Ivy itself may droop, there may be placed ferns or pressed autumn leaves above to help the effect with their gay colors.

Those cuttings which have rooted in water during the winter will need more plant food than this will supply. So in the spring, either plant them in the open border, or place them in pots, with soil, and they will soon become large plants.

Eight to ten large pots of Ivy trained over stakes and trellises, are at times used by some to ornament a single room.

Hanging baskets are sometimes constructed entirely without soil—holding only moss. A quantity of vials are filled with water and placed therein so as to be well concealed; slips of Ivy are inserted in some of these vials; Ferns are interspersed in other bottles, and cut flowers added to others; brilliant autumn leaves pressed and varnished are added here and there. All combined make a very choice parlor ornament. The only care needed is to keep the water replenished as long as it will last.

In the previous chapter on hanging baskets may be seen a design of a very handsome combination of Ferns and climbing Ivy, in Fig. 4, and in Fig. 11, is a sketch of the Ivy as we see it in its most familiar habits of growth. The bowl is an earthen one, such as now are imported and found on sale at most floral stores. A single cutting has been placed in here, and now it is branching out ward vigorously.

The directions for propagating Ivy from slips or cuttings, are very simple. Take a young, tender branchlet, cut about three inches in length, and insert half an inch of its stem in wet sand, or soil, under a bell glass or tumbler. Keep the soil well moistened, and yet warm, by placing it in the sunshine for fully a week. Then loosen the sand, withdraw the stem, and if rootlets have started, put immediately in a pot of good garden earth, mixed with one-third its quantity of sand Press the soil firmly about this young plant, to the same height as the sand reached before, cover with the bell glass again, and set in the *shade* for a week, then set the glass aside and bring to the sunshine. It should be watered frequently, but only just enough to keep it from wilting Early in June, if it has grown too long, trim off the large branches, set it out doors in the garden, then in September, again put it in a large pot with newer soil, bring to a cool and shady room at first, then gradually bring it to the heat.

There are several varieties of the Ivy, commonly grown by all gardeners. The *Hedera helix* is the English Ivy, the common outdoor climbing variety, found in all parts of Europe. It is of slow growth, two feet a year out doors being considered good progress. It needs water more freely than any of the other sorts, for drouth is death to it. It may be propagated by first cutting slips, then rooting them in bottles of water, and afterward transferring with sand.

The *Hedera Canariensis*, is the Irish Ivy, slightly larger than the others; leaves five lobed. Will thrive in a cool, shady, and close room. Too great exposure to the heat of the sun will cause the leaves to turn purple, or ripen too quickly; yet it will seldom blossom without sunshine. The flower is very ordinary, and it is more to be prized for its elegant light green foliage, which are thrown out from its luxuriant shoots.

The German Ivy is not properly of this family, but its botanical name is *Senecio Scandens*. This grows much more rapidly than either of the above, has lighter green leaves, and is entirely free from troublesome insects. Its branches trail in long festoons. Whether grown in the hanging basket, or over the window, it will soon wreath it with its leafy canopy. It may be trained as a pyramid by inserting stakes in the pots, and then letting the vine curve around toward the top, or it may be trained as an umbrella, or bushes, or on a semicircle, or any form that the frame is made to take. Its easy propagation—for every slip will take root— quick growth, have made it a favorite with every one.

Another variety called the Coliseum Ivy, (*Linaria cymbalaria,*) is also popular. It grows in slender purplish stems, having small green leaves with purple linings, and its flowers are like those of the Antirrhinum, but are very minute, being of lilac, white and yellow tints, mingled together. It grows in cracks or crevices of old buildings, and the roof of the grand Cathedral at Milan, is thickly overgrown with it in patches. It seeds plentifully, sows itself, and is also most easily propagated by cuttings. The soil most suitable for it is light sandy loam, yet it does not endure much moisture or dampness.

There are still a dozen or fifteen other varieties to be obtained in this country, each peculiar in itself, yet, the variegated varieties, *marginata, argentea,* &c., are the most desirable. They exist in many different forms, all variously margined with creamy, silver, or yellow colors—on the leaves. They are used either for climbers on the walls, or in beds, as margins. They do best when fully exposed to the sunshine, and in a comparatively poor soil. Under the name of Silver Edge Ivy, the *argentea* has been used for edging flower beds and for terrace gardens, having a broad margin of silvery white,—other varieties have three colors, white, green, and rose, or yellow.

The list of varieties exceeds fifty in number, some producing gigantic leaves of thick texture, others white or golden berries, some richly variegated, others with small leaves of deepest purple. They form a study of deepest interest, and many should be better known; yet strange to say, in the majority of the florists Catalogues, a few only are mentioned for popular cultivation, the German the Coliseum, and the variegated *L'elegante.*

CHAPTER XII.

CLIMBING VINES—BALCONY GARDENING.

What delicate taste and suggestive beauty seem gathered up in the associations of climbing vines.

Helps to Home Adornment we have often called them, and the fairy fingers who twine them around their parlor windows, or along the piazza, or on the rustic trellis before the cottage door, will tell you how well they appreciate their value in making home so pleasant. Climbing vines afford us an opportunity of clothing not the outside of the window alone, but its inside also, with verdure and decorations of greenery, for our imagination must now include, as part of the domain of house-gardening, the ornature of the outside of the window, piazza, or balcony, as well as the interior. Ideas of refinement, taste and beauty, are invariably suggested by the presence of climbing vines. Let the corners of our houses, or the edges of our windows, be hid under the delicate foliage or brilliant flowers, and their natural festoons of mingled verdure and bloom will soften the most gloomy surroundings

Our new built houses, with all their architectural finish and imposing design, still lack the last softening polish which comes only from the mellowing and genial touch of the vine. The first thing to be considered in growing vines indoors is the *soil*. Bulbous plants require light and very loose soil. Short, fibrous roots need a firm, fine soil. Long and spreading roots need a heavier and coarser soil than others. For most plants good garden loam, loosened, when necessary, by mixing with it street sand or gravel, and enriched by the application of a liquid stimulant answers very well. To make this stimulant, mix half a peck of stable manure or street sweepings, with a quart of pulverized charcoal, in a three-gallon vessel, and fill up the vessel with soft water. After it has stood a week the vessel will be ready for use. It should be clear. Water your plants with this three days consecutively, once in three weeks, during their earliest growth and blooming. It should be perfectly odorless; if not, then add more charcoal. As the liquid becomes more exhausted add more water. This quantity of fertilizing material will supply stimulant enough for two dozen large plants during six months

If you can obtain leaf mould—the fine, dark soil from the woods—take this for a third ingredient of your soil. It will prove, also, quite as nutritive as this fertilizer. If fertilizing liquids are used, they must be applied directly to the soil; but when water only is used, the whole plant should be showered with it, if possible

In selecting our list we have regard naturally to those which are most rapid growers.

First on the list is *Coboea scandens.* It is an old favorite, and it is worthy of remark, that but few of the novelties introduced of late years can equal some of the "*old favorites*" which we have long been accustomed to grow.

The vine is named from Cobo, a Spanish priest, who first cultivated it in Mexico, where he found it growing wild, and rambling in full luxuriance and beauty. A new variety of this vine, (Coboea scandens folius variegata) is much the most suitable for in-door culture.

The growth of the vine is very rapid, and it is equally easy of cultivation; the only essentials to success being warmth, a rich, though light soil, and sufficient water. If allowed to become very dry it will wither away. It requires sun and a warm room for it to grow in perfection; yet it is not a tender plant; *i. e.*, it will live anywhere, provided the frost does not touch it, and is one of the few plants which will flourish luxuriantly in parlors lighted with gas and kept at almost fever heat.

If grown in a hanging basket or pot, it must be large, and the roots allowed plenty of room to spread out in. In the summer the pots can be removed from the interior room to a balcony or piazza, or plunged into the ground until they are again wanted. Then clip off the growth of branches and leaves; place the pot back again in a sunny window, where it will soon start forth afresh, with new leaves and arms to cover the window

Its flowers are two inches long, and bell-shaped. At first their coloring is of a greenish hue, but it changes to a rich bluish-purple, and will continue in bloom for a week or more. Its calyx is large, and the long stamens seemingly grow at one side of it, giving to the flower much grace. It is easily raised from cuttings and seeds. The latter require some special care. If planted in the open ground they will generally decay; hence, pot or hot-bed culture is necessary. Usually the seeds are sown in March or April in light, rich soil, in pots, warmed with a gentle heat. After they have started, the young plants, when two inches high, are potted separately into small pots, and when they have grown about a foot high are carried to the place where they are to remain Usually there is no difficulty in the greenhouse or conservatory, where they are produced abundantly. Amateurs who cannot propagate them will do well to buy them from the florist already started.

It is one of the best of vines for parlor decoration, as it will drape and festoon the window, and stretch forth its tendrils, running up even to the ceiling. The tendrils are so clinging in their nature that they will attach themselves to anything which comes within their reach—curtain cords, branches of other plants, brackets, &c., throwing out new branches everywhere.

Smilax.

The Smilax (Medeola asparagoides) is now seen in almost every window basket, cultivated extensively for its rich, wavy, glossy foliage. For table decorations, wreaths, festoons, &c., it is very popular, and in all festive occasions where green drapery is used the Smilax occupies a prominent part—always considered indispensable. It is a bulb, a native of the Cape of Good Hope, and requires a rich but rather sandy soil to grow in perfection, also a liberal use of liquid manure, and when in a growing state must have plenty of water. Its leaves are in reality its branches; its flowers are of a whitish green, and its berries, or seed-pods, black; but it is cultivated entirely for its graceful sprays. These are often injured by their deadly enemies, the red spiders. By giving the plants a good shower of water once a week they will soon be free from the insects, or if this is not convenient, dust them with red pepper.

The Smilax does not require a very sunny location, but will thrive in a partly shaded window or on a bracket. It propagates itself by offsets from the parent bulb; yet it can also be raised from seeds. It requires some support to cling to, and will run more rapidly if a wire is fastened around the outside edge of the pot, and to this let there be attached small cords an inch or two apart. Fasten the ends of the cords together at the top of the ceiling, and on these slight supports the vines will closely twine.

In the summer give it but little water, and keep it in the shade where it will remain dormant. In September repot in fresh soil, and give occasional stimulants.

It is one of our most delicate vines for the parlor; a great favorite with every one, for its graceful leaves form a very pleasant effect when trained either around the basket, or pictures or statuary.

Tropæolums.

The varieties of this class are very numerous—all beautiful and handsome objects for either indoor or garden use. They are all rapid growers during the winter months, and are usually propagated from seeds, which produce a great variety of colors; one especial advantage being the fact of their flowering the first season so soon after planting. For ornamenting the window, or the green-house, or for covering the trellis, arbor, or balcony, they are admirably suited on account of their dense foliage and fine bloom.

Tropæolum Lobbianum, is better suited for window use, than the open ground. Flowers are of very bright orange and scarlet colors, and vine a very vigorous grower; propagated best from cuttings.

The *Tropæolum tricolorum*, is a bulbous-rooted climber, and best suited for the green-house or conservatory. It should be planted in September to enable it to obtain a good start before the winter starts in. Plant the tubers, which are not unlike a potato, eye upwards, and about an inch and a half beneath the surface of the pot, which should be eight to nine inches in diameter, and filled up with a light but rich soil. Give a little water when you plant it, and set the pot in a warm but rather shady spot, not letting the soil become dry; until you see the shoots starting freely give but little water, then give water daily. When the branches appear, train them to a trellis, or archway, according to your taste. A plant of the *tricolorum* can be placed on one side of the archway or trellis, with its crimson, orange and black blossoms to contrast with some of the other varieties, either *Lobbianum* or *peregrinum*

Tropaeolum pentaphyllum, a beautiful kind of Tropaeolum; like the tri-color, but not robust in habit. This kind will come to a great perfection if planted in a large pot and placed on a balcony

Tropaeolum trimaculatum, an annual species of more tender growth than Trop-major. It can be raised from seeds, and will give in their treatment during the summer season, a good series. Many flowers and a graceful growth is the character of this plant.

Sandy loam, with a third of decomposed manure well mixed with it, will grow the slower growing varieties to best advantage; for those more rapid, we would not admit more than one fourth manure When the leaves and flowers begin to fade away, and turn yellow and sere, give but very little water, and when dying down give none at all, but remove the bulbs from the pots, and keep them in sand in a cool place until another September comes around. They propagate themselves by tubers, which can be divided, and also will root easily from cuttings, which will form roots in vases of water; if the branches are full of buds when placed in the vases, they will bloom finely, and form a very pretty ornament for the parlor or sitting-room. Put bits of charcoal into the glasses, and the water will keep sweet and pure.

Maurandia

The *Maurandia Barclayana* is an exceedingly pretty climber for indoors. It grows readily from seed or cuttings. If from the latter, they should be started in June, so as to make a strong plant by autumn.

If grown from seed, plant in light, rich soil, in June; water it freely, and give plenty of sun. It blossoms profusely, hanging out full of elegant white, purple, or pink bell-shaped flowers, which much resemble those of the *Foxglove*. It needs a fertilizer once a week, from the time the buds first appear till blooming is past.

It is a vine of the easiest growth and culture, winding about slender strings or supports in the window, and in two or three months' time it will cover a small trellis anywhere with its graceful branches and pretty flowers. Seeds can be obtained of most florists, which will furnish all colors of violet, white, scarlet, rose, and purple.

Thunbergia.—This is another ornamental climber, easily raised from seed. It grows in any good garden soil, and will soon cover a window frame. It is really a greenhouse perennial, and is propagated by cuttings for greenhouse use. In the open ground its seed is usually sown about the last of May; grows freely, about six feet high; has many side branches, and needs a trellis to cling to; flowers are usually a buff or white color, with a rich maroon colored throat Other varieties have shades of orange and yellow.

The Passion Flower.

The *Passion Flower*, is one of our old standard varieties, much cultivated and admired, and very desirable for parlor ornament. It thrives best in light, rich soil, and needs much sunlight to bloom in profusion. It cannot bear great water-

Fig. 18.—*Passiflora cærulea*, Blue Passion Flower.

ing: only be sure that the leaves will not droop from dryness, and it will flourish. Plant the seed, or start cuttings in moist sand, in the greenhouse. After a plant has got a vigorous growth, it may be brought into the parlor, and remain as long as it is warm.

Passiflora cærulea, has flowers of a sky blue color and remarkable character; grows finely, and is quite ornamental. It should be pruned close back to within a bud or two of the main stem every summer or autumn, as it blooms on the shoots from these buds during the next season. It can usually be had of the florist, and may be kept as a plant for the Conservatory. If planted out to ornament a veranda or trellis, it must be protected during the winter, by covering over, as it will not stand the frost. It climbs twenty feet or more, and is quite handsome. For house culture take pot plants already started; keep in a temperature of 60° to 75°. Several other varieties are suitable also:—

Passiflora racemosa.   *Passiflora quadrangularis.*
" *permessina.*   " *princeps.*

A fine variegated variety has been produced—trifasciata; its dark green, tricolored leaves having a broad band of deep rose color through the various centres. Its foliage is very handsome, and its flowers being of the usual color, makes it very desirable

For training in conservatories, they are among the most effective of all ornamental climbers, producing a great profusion of blooms.

Ipomœa. The Morning Glory.

These have proved with many ladies the easiest and simplest of all vines to raise indoors. They are raised chiefly from the seeds, and will usually grow sufficiently well to bloom in four to six weeks after planting. They are very rapid climbers, and much more delicate than the Convolvulus to which they are closely allied. The principal varieties suitable for indoors are:

I. coccinea, (Star Ipomœa,) with small scarlet flowers.
I. limbata, white margin, bluish centre, in the form of a star.

The Ivy.

This has been mentioned in a chapter by itself. For basket purposes the *German Ivy*, or *Coliseum Ivy*, will naturally be chosen first; but for climbing purposes, around the windows or doors of the room, choose the *Hedera helix*, *English Ivy*, or the *Canariensis Irish Ivy*, which will be sure to grow in any room. Both should be frequently watered.

Cissus discolor

Is a greenhouse climber, with finely variegated leaves, which are in great demand in the cities for the margins of baskets of flowers. It will hardly grow well in a window garden, as it needs the highest temperature of a forcing house to develope its beauties; but in a proper location it will be for a short time a great addition to a collection of plants. It will grow during the summer in the windo w if shaded; but will not in the winter, unless it has a great deal of heat and light.

Clerodendron Balfouri

Needs a warm temperature. Its flowers are of a bright scarlet, with a calyx of pure white, and the clusters are six inches in diameter. It blooms for many months during the winter, and is invaluable for bouquets and roses. It requires a rich soil and much sunshine, but it will grow well in a southeastern location.

The list of climbing vines is very extensive For parlor culture it seems hardly necessary to make any addition to a list in which there are so successful and popular favorites as the Ivy, Cobœa, and Morning Glory.

Most of the climbing vines suitable for indoor growth are generally grown in the greenhouse. Often they are started in large pots or boxes, and when trained to a trellis are transferred to a warm sitting-room to stand there as objects of ornament; but few undertake to grow greenhouse climbers there for permanent use.

List of Climbing Plants most useful for the Parlor, Window, or Balcony Decoration.

a. Annual, bi-annual, or such species and varieties with tender and soft vines
Maurandya Barclayana, Lareyana, and other varieties.
Cardiospermum Halicacaba, baloon vine.
Tropaeolum majus, and *majus fl. pleno.*
   trimaculatum.
   Lobbianum, and its hybrids.
Cyclanthera pedato, and *p. explodens.*
Adlumia cirrhosa, (*Fumaria fungosa.*)
Thunbergia alata, and *T. aurantiaca.*
Lophospermum scandens, and varieties.
Pilogyne suavis.
Ipomœa quamoclit, and *quamoclit alba.*
   coccinea, and *coccinea lutea.*
Obobra viridiflora.
Scyphanthus elegans.
Loasa lateritia.
Callistega pubescens flore pleno.
Manettia bicolor.
   cordifolia, (*coccinea.*)
Micania scandens, (*Senecio micanoides.*)
   b. Running plants with a more ligneous habit
Clematis azurea grandiflora, and new hybrids.
   flammula. and *C. lanuginosa.*
Passiflora incarnata, (hardy perennial.)
   edulis fol. var.

Passiflora caerulea, and *caerulea varieties.*
  trifasciata.
  kermesina.
  princeps.
  quadrangularis.
Cobœa scandens, and *scandens fol. var.*
Thunbergia laurifolia, and *T. grandiflora*
Medeola asparagoides, (*Myrsophyllum.*)
Mikania speciosa Verschaffeltii and *Warcsewitzii.*
Akebia quinata.
Phaseolus Caracalla.
Physianthus albens.
Ipomœa digitata, (*palmata*)
  ficifolia and *insignis.*
  Hlorsfalliae.
  tyrianthina.
Stigmaphyllom ciliatum.
Solanum jasminoides.
Tecoma jasminoides.
Mimosa prostrata.
Bignonia venusta, and *speciosa.*
  argyraea—*violacea* and *ornata.*
Tacsonia mollissima, and *T. Van Volxemii.*
Rhyncospermum jasminoides, and *var.*
Tropæolum tri-colorum, and *T. pentaphyllum.*
Cissus discolor.
  antarcticus.
Rubus Moluccanus.
Stephanotus floribundus.
Ampelopsis Veitchii, and *quinquefol, fol. var.*
Lonicera brachypoda aureo reticulata.

Balcony Gardening.

When the warm suns of spring and summer make the air more genial, our taste for outdoor gardening returns, and the first step after leaving the window garden is to embellish our balcony or veranda. To this spot we bring our hanging baskets and suspend them between the overhanging arches, or fasten upon one of the piazza supports a hollow bracketed vessel. Throw therein some soil, and try a trailing plant or two. In the grassy border just beneath we sow the seeds of some of our most rapid and cleanly growing hardy vines, which will cover the balcony soon with their dense shade.

To those disposed to try a little amateur gardening, and willing to undergo considerable pains and care, we recommend a series of boxes wherein may be grown plants of ornamental foliage, such as Coleus, Achyranthes, Ferns, or into which you may transfer your pot plants from inside the window. These boxes may be usually made of pine wood, painted green, and vary from six to eight inches deep, and ten to fifteen inches wide. Fill up all the interspace not occupied by the pots with sand; also fit castors to the boxes, so that they may be easily moved from one part to the other. Into these boxes may be set trellises, and upon them may be trained the Fuchsia, Ivy, Clematis, or Morning Glory. Different boxes may be used for different classes of plants: one for Geraniums, another for Ferns, a third for Ivy, a fourth for Roses, a fifth for Evergreens, (the Arbor Vitæ being best,) another for Bulbs, (Tuberoses, Lilies, &c., being best.) The length of these boxes should not exceed four feet.

Mignionette boxes are generally made 7 inches deep, 7 inches wide, and from 1½ to 3 feet long. Mignionette looks best when the plants are grown *en masse*, and for this there must be depth of soil. It is not a bad plan to plant a few climbers in the boxes, so that when the Mignionette fades away the vines will fill up the blank space.

Tom Thumb Tropaeolums, Canary Bird Flower, Asters, Stocks, Balsams, are all very suitable for this style of box and balcony gardening.

Zonale Geraniums, Pelargoniums, of all kinds will do well. Plants of variegated foliage, like the Abutilon, need a slightly shaded locality

Heliotropes, Salvias, Verbenas, &c., require a strong exposure to sun and air, and will bloom well in a southeastern exposure.

In a western balcony the variegated leaved Ivy Geranium, scarlet, white, and pink; Tom Thumb Geraniums, and Mignionette, will bloom most perfectly. Ivies will twine about the frame-work, no matter what may be the exposure, but the Madeira vine likes a warm place, and the Smilax anywhere.

Fuchsias desire the shade; hence, a northerly exposure, except when too cool, will suit them; also the Pansies, Myrtles, and Funkia variegata do best there.

Brackets may be fitted to the sides of the window frame, and in them placed pots filled with drooping flowers, like the Colisseum Ivy and *Tradescantia zebrina*.

At a slight expense you might construct a small hanging garden, similar to one of the designs illustrated in the chapter for hanging baskets, and suspend it at the end of the piazza. You may also introduce vases upon your veranda with good effect; but for this you do not need tall plants. The most effective flowers are those of Pansies, Verbenas, and Petunias.

Balcony gardening in winter is of course an impossibility, unless we make exceptions in favor of a few Evergreens. These are suitable at all seasons of the year, and nothing is more neat and tasteful, requiring less care than a box of Arbor Vitæs, for these are much easier to grow than Pines or Spruces.

If the balcony is limited in space, do not attempt bushy plants, and shrubs will be out of place. Here climbing vines are the most appropriate.

But if you do have plenty of room you may introduce in the spring such shrubby plants as the *Azalea*, the *Weigela rosea*, and the *Spirea prunifolia*. A

Fig. 19.—Design for Balcony Garden.

WINDOW GARDENING.

gay display can be made by arranging two boxes, one with the Lobelia in front, and behind it a row of scarlet Geraniums, such as the *Gen. Grant, Warrior,* or *Marie Lemoine.* For a dwarf Geranium the *Tom Thumb* is best. The *Delphinium formosum* is good also for the balcony. Cut away the blooms as fast as they get done. In order to keep the plants in good health and growth, it would be well to see that the soil of the boxes or pots is covered with moss, and once a day, in the evening or early morning, give the plants a thorough syringing of water, for upon the dry floor of the balcony evaporation will be quite rapid in warm days. Seeds of the *Mignionette, Sweet Alysum, Phlox Drummondii,* and *Nemophila* will all do well.

Nothing is so effective as the Scarlet Sage, Salvia Splendens, gorgeous with its dazzling beauty.

A good plant or two of the Dielytra will make a showy box, and then you can make room for a few Verbenas, Petunias, Larkspurs, and Heliotropes. We would not recommend any bulbs, such as the Gladiolus; except the Lilium Aurtum, which will often do well; also the Lilium Longiflorum.

If you wish to grow bulbs and make a fine display, you must remove your boxes from the balcony just before winter; fill them with appropriate soil, (such as is named in chapter on Bulbs,) sink them in the garden border, plant in it your bulbs of Hyacinths, Tulips, Crocuses, Snow Drops, &c., to remain during the winter, well covered with some mulch. In early spring take them up, replace again upon the balcony, and allow them to grow and bloom. This is a very good plan where a box of flowering bulbs is desired for the jam just outside of the window-sill. After flowering the box may be filled up again with bedding plants. Every evening give a good sprinkling of water, and once a week you may add a dose of liquid fertilizer to all your plants on the balcony. In very hot weather watering may be given twice a day, remembering the only safe rule, never to give it between the hours of 9 A. M. and 4 P. M., while the sun's rays are warmest; hence, affording the most danger. Where balconies are enclosed by glass screens upon all sides they become house conservatories, and admit of the same management which is given to plants for window or greenhouse culture. Plants of greater variety may be admitted here during all seasons of the year, but usually nearly everything is removed from them during the summer months, and placed outdoors to enjoy the fresh air and invigorating rains.

The *Aucuba Japonica* is a handsome evergreen shrub; flowers are of no value, being small, but the leaves are large, of a glossy green, blotched with a pale yellow color, tapering off to white. It must be grown in a partially shaded location, as it cannot bear the hot rays of the sun. It is hardy, and will withstand ordinary winters.

Vines for the Balcony.

In these you will find your most effective means of decoration. Most of the hardy garden favorites will grow from 30 to 50 feet in a season, and a great merit is their earliness and frequency of bloom. The list suitable for this purpose is quite large, so we name only the best six or eight.

Fig. 20.—A Cottage Porch, with Climbing Vines at the Side.

The *Honeysuckle* might almost be called a *vine of romance*. It has been so celebrated in words of sentiment or gems of poetry. The Japan variety (Lonicera brachypoda) is much the best; leaves are large, of a bright green color; flowers of a delicate sweet fragrance. As a vine for covering arbors, pillars, trellises, balconies, &c., it is unsurpassed.

The *Trumpet Honeysuckle* (*Lonicera sempervirens*,) is one of the species of the Woodbine, so well known for its beauty of flower, and high fragrance. This species is referred to by *The Agriculturist* as one of the native varieties; not as showy as some of the later varieties, has fine dark green leaves, flowers tubular, about two inches long, of a fine scarlet outside, yellow within and very brilliant. It multiplies from either layers or cuttings; will not do well north of New York, but is very suitable for the Southern States.

The *Wistaria* has the merit of permanency. Its stems, once grown and trained, do not die down yearly, but remain, and grow even more luxuriant and profuse in bloom year after year. It is quite hardy; will stand our winters without much protection. The flowers are of a light blue color, and bloom almost constantly during the summer months, although the principal period is in May; is grown from cuttings or layers. Cultivators will do best to buy a good plant already well started.

The *Scarlet Trumpet Creeper* (*Bignonia grandiflora*) has much the showiest flowers of all the hardy climbing vines; flowers are of rich scarlet, produced in the greatest profusion, blooming only in July and August. It will attach itself firmly to anything it can reach, and throw out innumerable little rootlets, which do not let go their hold. It is a very rapid grower, and its appearance is very much heightened by the contrast of the flowers with the bright, glossy, deep green of the leaves.

The *Aristolochia sipho*, or *Dutchman's Pipe*, is a very curious vine, with leaves possessing an almost tropical appearance, being of an extraordinary size, 8 to 10 inches broad. The flowers grow in the form of a small pipe, and possess little beauty. The plant is hardy, a rapid climber, and is particularly valuable for positions where a dense shade is quickly desired. Grown principally from cuttings.

The *Virginia Creeper*, or *American Ivy*, requires to be planted in rich, cool, moist soil. When well started it will grow with a rapidity unparalleled in native vines. Its foliage is its most valuable and interesting characteristic; during the summer time it is of a beautiful green, heightened in effect very materially by the festoons which swing off from the main stem, and add grace of habit to beauty of color. In the autumn the foliage, at the first advent of frost, is changed into the most brilliant of crimson colors, as if the vine were in a blaze of glory. It is best admired when seen in contrast with some other green vine close at hand, and hence, it is often twined with the Wisteria. The *Morning Glory*, (*Convolvulus major*,) with its brilliant, purple, crimson, or white flowers, is the easiest of all to raise from the seed, and always makes a fine display.

The *Tropæolum peregrinum*, (*Canary Bird Flower*,) is used for veranda purposes as well as for the garden or for bedding; flowers yellow; very ornamental growth about 10 feet.

It would be best to twine a different vine around each pillar or column and

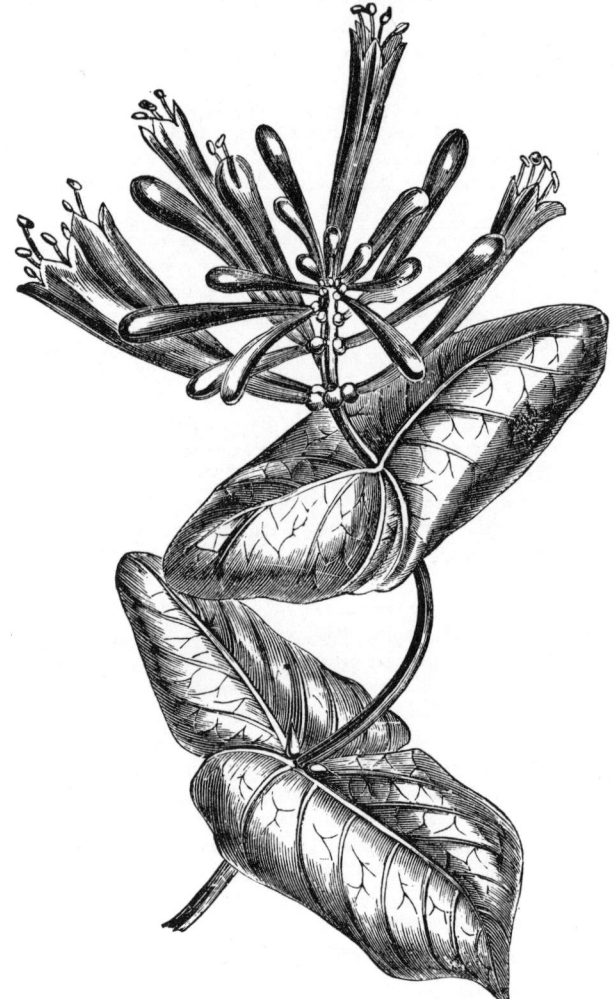

Fig. 21.—Trumpet Honeysuckle—*Lonicera sempervirens.*

some cases, where there will be a contrast of foliage and flowers, two different vines may be twined around the same column; but it is best to keep the annuals by themselves and the permanent varieties by themselves. The Clematis, Jasmine, or Climbing Roses may be added by those who have the taste. Indeed, we would recommend for a surety at least one Prairie Rose, either the Gem of the Prairies or the Queen of the Prairies, both of which are crimson in color, the former more durable and fragrant than the latter, but not as rapid a climber

House-top Gardening.

What a novelty! yet how reasonable the suggestion. In the German tale of the "*Old Mam'selle*," we read of its pleasures, and it is stated that in Sweden house-top gardens are not an uncommon sight, both in the country and in the villages. The roofs of some of the poorest cottages are covered with herbs, which afford a pasture for goats. In Norway they even plant trees in the turf which covers the roofs, and to such an extent is this carried that some of their hamlets or villages, seen at a distance, have quite the air of a little wood. Nothing is more common than to see rude kitchen gardens on these roofs of houses.

An English gentleman, writing to a London horticultural journal, mentions the pleasant recollections when he visited while a boy, over 50 years ago, the home of a French citizen, a Mr. Marquis, in Coleman street, London:

"This gentleman's hobby was a 'house-top garden' of the most complete and perfect character. At the lower part of the upper staircase was the root of a fine Sycamore, the foliage of which luxuriated in a 'glass house' above on the roof, amidst orange and lemon trees, with fairest flowers, tea, tobacco, and many other highly interesting specimens of vegetable life. I forget, at this distance of time, how many sorts of fruit were to be seen growing and flourishing in this 'house-top garden,' but the vine and its magnificent clusters of delicious grapes are ineffaceably engraved on memory's young tablets. Think of that, ye apathetic cockneys! hothouse grapes from Coleman street, and that not once in a day, but year after year, until the talented and spirited proprietor went to that bourne from whence no traveler returns, and then the master mind being gone the garden pined away.

"In a convenient corner of his elevated greenhouse Mr. Marquis had a lifting force-pump, with air vessel, to which a length of leather hose being attached, afforded a convenient means of watering and syringing the numerous plants collected in this unique garden."

This style of ornamental gardening is unusual here, and we remember but one instance of ever noticing an attempt to imitate it in this country. This was so successfully planned and executed that it will bear honorary mention.

In one of the principal streets of Louisville, Kentucky, may be seen a doctor's office, the roof of which is covered with a perfect mass of green plants in floral boxes. Directly in front, on the eaves just overhanging the front of the building, is a long box, about two feet wide, the same in height, and extending across the entire width of the top of the house. Here were planted a perfect mass of Verbenas and Portulaccas; at the corners were set drooping vines, which, as they grew, hung their long garlands of flowers away down before the lower win-

Fig. 22.—Aristolochia sipho, or Dutchman's Pipe.

dows. Just back of this was placed a wooden staging, with successive steps rising upward, covered with pots or boxes filled with plants of other character. Here were Fuchsias trained to a neat little trellis; Coleus in one pot; Achyranthes in another, and in one big tub had been planted a pumpkin seed, the vines from which sprawled all over the top of the staging and rustic arbor improvised overhead. Here and there, over the roof beyond, were put pots, each with a huge plant of the Ricinus fully eight feet high, and correspondingly broad. At each corner of the roof, also in the centre, and on an elevated stand near the front, were set big barrels or hogsheads full of water pumped up from below, and from holes at the bottom the water flowed through hose with sprinklers attached, and which sprinkled the plants at any time with a ready rain.

The Ricinus added vastly more than anything else to the decoration of the roof, by their stateliness and almost tropical beauty; but the trailing vines, with their garlands of bloom, helped out the symmetry and completed the grace of the whole. Scarcely a passer-by in the street but stopped long to look upon this novel scene; and the fame of the doctor's garden doubtless has been carried by strangers far beyond the borders of this lovely "*City of Flowers*."

Not long since a lady detailed to a delighted audience, of how she, with her sister, put to good practical use the roof of a one story L building, which was used for a kitchen. The roof was nearly flat, and afforded ready means for converting into a garden. Surrounding it with a wire trellis, they placed inside as many boxes, barrels, &c., as they could find. These they filled with rich dirt, manure, and street sweepings. Here they sowed seeds of Tomatoes, Cucumbers, Squash, Melons, String Beans, and anything of quick, easy growth. They actually did cultivate this curious garden for two years, and gathered, while each growing season lasted, excellent crops of vegetables, rich flavored, large and delicious; perhaps doubly appreciated in consequence of their being the fruit of their own labor. As long as it lasted the little series of box garden was well tilled, kept well watered with liquid manure, and was eminently successful. It ran down at last, owing to a change of occupants of the building.

A very pretty plan for a Rose Garden upon the top of a house has been suggested by a landscape gardener. Let the pillars and frame-work of the house be made very strong, capable of supporting a good weight of earth, &c. Then fill into earthern cribs all the rich earth that can be obtained to the depth of $1\frac{1}{2}$ feet, and cover the entire roof, except a path surrounding an oval bed in the centre. This path should be three feet wide. Here you may plant your Roses, Fuchsias, &c., in the open air, and they will, if kept well watered, bloom all the summer. The accompanying design and description, by Robert Morris Copeland, in an early number of "Hearth and Home," will explain itself:

"This little plan shows a roof 20 by 30 feet; provision must be made for a weight of 20 tons, for a cubic foot of soil weighs 100 pounds, and there are 900 cubic feet in the garden, or 600 square feet superficial area. This would crush an ordinary roof, so the weight must be lightened by taking out room for the path, and having only light weight in the centre figure

"Surround the roof with an iron frame 6 feet high, made of iron rods, set up at intervals of 6 feet, and connected with smaller rods running entirely around the roof. Train on this fence Wistaria, Woodbine, Honeysuckle, or Running Roses.

On the fence on the north side, where the Roses would get full sun, plant Baltimore Belle, Mrs. Hovey, or Rosa Ruga, if content with single blooming Roses; or select from the Noisettes La Marque or Aimee Vibert or Madame Henrietta, and from the Teas, Safrano.

On the east fence plant the *Lonicera Halliana*, Hall's Honeysuckle, and the Golden Berried Honeysuckle—all hardy; on the south, Golden and common Ivy; on the west, Dutch Monthly Honeysuckle and one running Rose

During the summer grow Tropæolum, Maurandia, Nierembergia, and Ipomœa among the hardy vines. In the northwest corner (*A*) set six Hybrid Perpetual Roses, then a bed of Heliotropes ; in the northeast corner six more Hybrid or other Perpetuals; *D* and *H*, occupied by roots of vines; cover the surface with Periwinkle, Nummularia, or Lycopodium ; *E*, June Roses: *F*, Tricolor Pelargoniums, which do best out of the direct rays of the sun; *G*, Moss Roses, single, blooming, and perpetual. In the centre bed *I* is a group of Coleus surunded by *Centauria candidissima ; J*, *K*, *L*, *M*, are filled with China, Bengal, and Tea Roses, the surface unoccupied to be covered with Blue Lobelia ; *X* is the trap door which leads out of the roof.

A roof garden for Roses could be planted every autumn with Bulbs, Snow drops, Crocuses, Hyacinths, and Tulips, all of which would blossom and die before the foliage of the Roses would be large enough to do any harm.

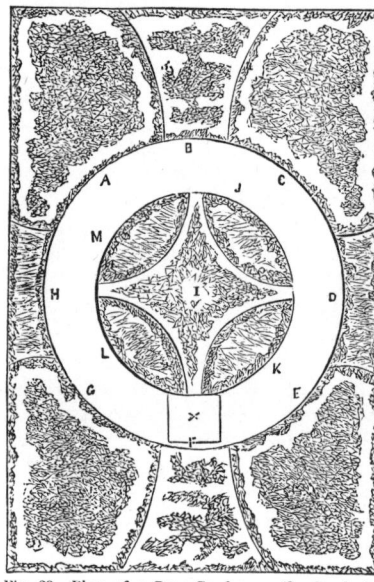

Fig. 23.—Plan of a Rose Garden on the Roof of a House.

Let, there be planted for instance, four colors of Hyacinths in the beds *J, K, L, M;* Crown Imperials and Tulips in *I;* border all the beds with Snowdrops; set Crocus in four colors inside of the Snowdrops ; fill *B, F, D, H* with mixed Tulips, and put Daffodils, Jonquils, and Polyanthus in *A, C, C, G.*

"The bed for roof gardens should be raised a few inches above the surface of the roof, the wood forming the bottom of the garden-box or crib, being perforated ; the sides of the box should be two feet high. First lay over the floor a few inches of leaves, broken bones, or coarse manure."

This idea of roof gardens may be still farther carried out, and made more permanently useful for winter as well as summer, by covering it all over with glass; then at any season of the year the flower-lover may repair here, and always be sure of finding some green things to enliven the looks, while in summer the glass may be opened to the admission of fresh air and rain.

If the amateur does not wish to go to so elaborate and expensive a construction, he may gratify his taste by the selection of large pots or boxes, fill them with soil, and then place them upon the roof, filled with appropriate plants.

Shrubs may be introduced here, such as the Deutzias, Spiraeas, or Weigelas but usually annual plants—*i. e.*, those grown from seed—will do the best, like Verbenas, Salvias, and climbing plants. Fuchsias, Heliotropes, and Geraniums will always be appropriate.

No prettier ornament to a house-top can be devised than to erect at each corner of the roof a pretty trellis. Let there be a rod or pole running across the vacant space from one trellis to the other; then at the bottom place a large tub of earth, and in it start a few plants of Ivy, or the Scarlet Trumpet Creeper, or the Wistaria. Keep them well watered, and their clambering tendrils, with their rich leaves, will soon festoon the arbor, and render the roof an inviting resort for all members of the family. The Ivy is much the simplest and safes ornament of this description to use, and the amateur had better not try any thing else until he becomes more familiar with plant-culture and can make good selection for himself.

CHAPTER XIII.

Bulbs.

Bulbous-rooted flowering plants are so numerous, conspicuous, and exquisitely beautiful, and withal so well adapted for the conservatory, that were all other plants annihilated or forgotten, this class alone would at all times fill the drawing-room with the most gorgeous as well as the most chaste and beautiful flowers, attractive not only for their delicacy, brilliancy, and variety of color, but as well for their most delightful fragrance. It is not our intention in this place to write a history of Bulbs, but merely to offer a few remarks on the adaptation and culture of the most desirable sorts, in connection with other classes of plants noticed in this work.

The Hyacinth.

Pre-eminent in this class stands the Hyacinth, which has been deservedly popular for more than three hundred years, and is to-day more sought after than any other species, simply because greater variety of color and quantity of bloom can be had with less trouble and expense than from any other. Hyacinths have a most generous nature; they will adapt themselves to almost any situation, and flower as freely and smile as sweetly in the poor man's window as in the more

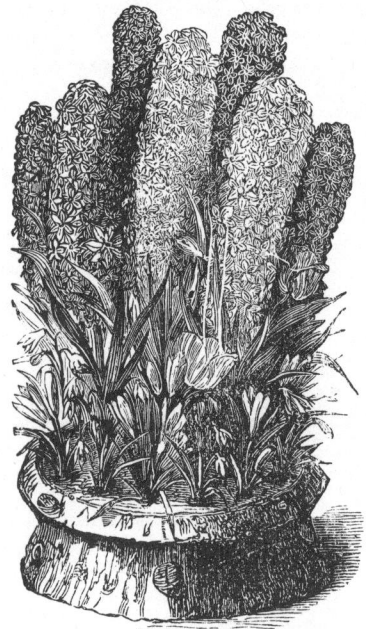

Fig. 24.—"Rustic Robin" Jardinet.

costly conservatory of the wealthy. While their generosity is so marked, their gratitude for, and appreciation of, attention shown them is equally marked. No plant pays so well for good culture as this; the difference between common planting and proper growing is so great that one would scarcely think or believe the flower could come from the same bulb. Hyacinths can be grown in a variety of ways. The best, simplest, and most common, is in pots. We shall, however describe the various ways we have grown them, and leave the reader to make his or her choice, as fancy may dictate.

First, a few words upon the selection of Bulbs are highly necessary. It may not be generally known that Hyacinths will not bloom *well* but once. In Holland, where they are only grown for market, they are not allowed to flower except in specimen beds, from the time the setts are planted until they are large enough to sell, which is usually when they are four years old. The flower-stalk is cut away as soon as it can be without damage to the foliage. This throws the whole strength of the plant into the bulb, which is kept growing until there is danger of its breaking, which the practiced eye of the grower readily sees. Then it is sent to market, and the next season will give the finest possible bloom, after which the old bulb will "break" and several small ones form, noen of which will ever do well enough to pay for growing the second season. We do not wish to mislead; this instruction is only for those who wish none but *first rate* flowers. Bulbs planted in the open border, after having bloomed in pots, will continue to bloom a number of years, but will give small, puny spikes, with but a few bells on each.

To flower bulbs successfully they should be procured as soon as possible after their arrival from Holland, which is generally about the first of September, and immediately potted in a soil composed of equal parts of good loam, leaf mould and well rotted cow manure, which should be well mixed,

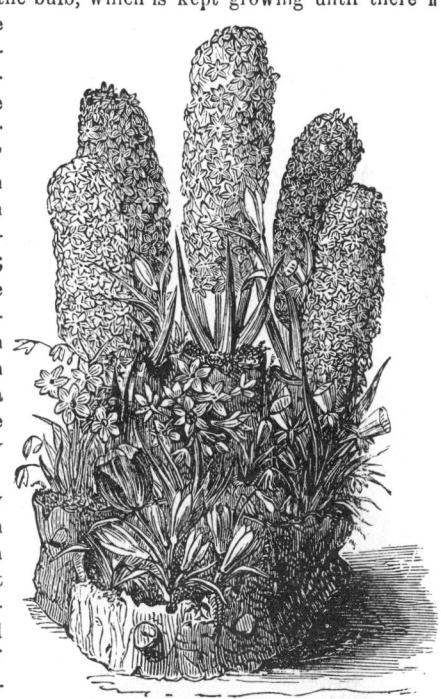

Fig. 25.—Princess Alexandra Jardinet.

after which add about one-fifth of good clean sand. No soil can be better than this for noble growth and bloom. The pots should be made on purpose ; not larger than five inches across, nor less than eight inches deep ; fill the pot nearly full of the compost, and press the bulb firmly in, so that the top of the bulb is about level with the top of the pot. After filling, they should be plunged in a frame or open border, and covered four inches with soil or some compost, where they should remain until the first of December. This operation is highly necessary to encourage the root growth, which must be made before the leaves shoot forth, for perfection of bloom. After the roots have reached the bottom of the pot, they may be brought into the conservatory to flower as wanted. Those brought in December 1st, will bloom by New Years. Water should be freely given them as soon as they begin to grow, but do not soak them, neither allow them to dry up. Even temperature, even watering, with plenty of fresh air, are the essentials for their well growing. As soon as the flower-stem is fully developed, one or two waterings with liquid manure is highly beneficial. The style of growth, and the size of the flowers and trusses of plants cultivated in this manner, will very much excel those grown in the ordinary way, and will amply repay the care bestowed. The same soil and treatment should be given them if planted in boxes, Jardinieres, tubs, or any device the grower may select.

Fig. 26.—" Prince of Wales" Jardinet.

Hyacinths can be and are commonly grown in glasses. One or two seasons generally satisfy the enthusiast, however, that it is not the better way. Many will every year try this method, and for such the following instructions will be most likely the ones to insure success. The ordinary Hyacinth glass will answer, but Tye's pattern is decidedly preferable. Always use rainwater; put them in the glasses about the first of October; do not fill above the bottom of the bulb. It is better not to let the water quite reach the bulb. After filling, place in a dark closet until the roots reach the bottom of the glass, which will generally be in about three weeks; be careful to keep away from frost; change the water as often as it becomes discolored, and fill up to the bottom of the bulb any time there is a vacancy between the periods of change. When they begin to grow, give them all the light possible without setting them where they will get the noonday sun. A friend once called us to see and tell him why his Hyacinths did not " do well." Upon examination we found the water hot from the sun; not merely warm, but hot enough to cook the bulb, which is not the way they should be served up. To set the glasses on the window ledge is nearly as fatal to them; the cold air coming up between the sash chills them. Plants of all kinds are as sensitive to a draft as human beings are. In order to have them near the light, put up light brackets or a narrow shelf across the window, say six inches from the glass, which will protect them both from the sun and the draft.

A very good plan for growing them in glasses is first to put the bulb in clean sand until the roots have become well grown, say six inches long; then take them out of the sand, put them in glasses, and treat as above. It is really curious to see them growing in water, and when, as you sometimes will do, you get a good spike, the satisfaction is very great.

Hyacinths will grow and bloom in moss alone, if it be kept continually wetted; but a far better way is to fill half way whatever vessel you may choose—a bowl, dish, or vase—with clean sand, place the bulb upon it, and fill the rest with good green moss. Use sufficient water to keep the sand full, but with none lying on the top. Once in three or four waterings you may use liquid manure, which may be made of half a peck of well rotted cow manure put in ten gallons of water, well stirred up, and allowed to settle, the clear liquid alone being used. This will strengthen the growth; still without such stimulant the plants will come short, strong, and well colored, if kept fully exposed to the light, and well supplied with air.

Fig. 27.—Jardinet, with Hyacinth.

Those who grow Hyacinths in part to gratify curiosity, will be amused by taking a deep saucer or glass dish, fill it to the rim with clean, white gravel, upon which place a good, firm bulb; then treat the same as with glasses. The roots will soon fill the dish, running over and through the gravel, forming a solid mass.

SELECTION OF VARIETIES.

As a rule, we prefer the single varieties for forcing. But few of the double ones produce a fine truss, the bells being uneavenly and thinly scattered along the stem. For glasses, moss, or saucers, the single ones must be selected. With the following sorts we have generally been successful:

DOUBLE RED.—*Bouquet Royal,* large, rosy bells; a good bloomer.
Bouquet Tender, fine, deep red; one of the best reds
Comptesse de La Costa, very fine dark rose, with good spike

Fig. 28.—Ornamental Hyacinth Glasses.   Fig. 29.—Tye's Triple Hyacinth Glass.

Duke of Wellington, very fine pale rose; the bells large and beautifully arranged, often giving two spikes.
Grootforst, pale rose; good spike, with nicely shaped bells.
Regina Vic'oria, bright pink; large bells, and fine spike.

DOUBLE WHITE—*Anna Maria,* fine, waxy white, with pink eye; good formed bells and spike.
Jenny Lind, blush white, with purple eye; good bells; compact truss.

La Deese, pure white, finely-shaped bells, but thin spike.
La Vestale, lily white; small bells and spike.
Prince of Waterloo, fine, pure white; large bells; moderate spikes.

DOUBLE BLUE—*Blocksberg*, fine bright and marbled blue; very large bells and spike.

Fig. 30.—Ornamental Vase for Bulbs.

Grande Vidette, fine porcelain blue; large bells and spike.
Laurens Koster, beautiful bright indigo, large bells. and first rate form, with an immense spike.
Lord Wellington, clear blue; dark centre; good form.
Prince Frederick, fine porcelain blue; large bells and spike

DOUBLE YELLOW—*Bouquet d' Orange*, fine citron yellow; small bells; moderate spike.
Jaunne Supreme, fine, clear yellow ; good spike.

SINGLE RED—*Diebitz Sabalskansy*, bright red, moderate bells, and good spike.
Duke of Wellington, fine rose; large bells and spike.
L'Ami du Cœur, deep pink; small bells ; moderate spike.
Madame Hodgson, pale pink, good bells, and finely-formed spike.
Norma, a magnificent waxy pink ; immense bells and spike.
Robert Steiger, fine, deep crimson, large bells, and immense spike.

Fig. 31.—Ornamental Vase for Bulbs.

Fig. 32.—Tye's Single Hyacinth Glass.

SINGLE WHITE—*Elfrida*, creamy blush; very large bells; immense spike.
Grand Vainquer, pure white; fine bells and spike; extra.
Grand Vidette, pure white, large bells, and long spike; very early.
Grand Blanche Imperiale, fine blush; moderate bells; large spike.

Grandeur a Merville, very fine, pale blush, good bells, and immense spike.

Mont Blanc, beautiful, clear white; large bells; immense spike.

Victoria Regina, very fine, pure white, large, waxy bells, and fine spike.

Voltaire, very beautiful blush · large bells; compact spike; of immense size.

SINGLE BLUE—*Baron Van Tuyll,* fine, dark porcelain; large bells; extra fine spike.

Charles Dickens, fine, pale blue; large bells; very fine spike.

Grand Lilas, beautiful, delicate azure blue; large, perfect bells; immense spike; one of the best.

Grand Vidette, fine, pale blue, immense bells, and moderate spike.

Nimrod, beautiful, pale blue; large bells and spike.

Orandates, very fine porcelain blue, large bells, and very fine spike.

Porcelain Sceptre, very fine, pale blue; moderate bells; very fine spike.

SINGLE YELLOW—*Anna Carolina,* beautiful, clear yellow; handsome bells and spike.

Heroine, pale yellow, with green tips; large truss.

Roman White Hyacinth,

A new variety lately introduced; a most valuable acquisition for early blooming, suitable only for pots. The bells of this variety are very small, not more than half the size of the Dutch bulbs. They can be grown in three-inch pots; same soil as recommended for the other sorts. If planted in September, they can be made to bloom by the 1st of December. Flowers pure white, very fragrant, small bells, and spike; each bulb will give from three to five spikes. For early flowering it is indispensable.

We cannot leave this interesting class of plants without a word of caution to those about selecting bulbs. Do not buy cheap bulbs, neither those that are very high priced, because of their scarcity. Good bulbs cannot be had at less than three dollars per dozen; that is, such bulbs as ought to be grown in the "window." Avoid "mixed" bulbs, which are simply culls. In Holland, when the crop is harvested, the *very best* are selected and sent to England and France, where the prices are twice as much as here; the next choice is for this and other markets, sold under *Named sorts;* the next grade are put up and sold in separate colors; the balance of stock is sold at auction, to be put up in "cases" for auction in this country, or hawked about our streets by German pedlars. Go to a reliable seedsman, and if you do not know what you want, take his advice.

Tulips.

Few flowers have received the marked attention, and been so universally grown and admired, as the Tulips. But few plants are so varied in their characters, and scarcely a family so large but what has more poor relations. No class of plants has so many superb varieties. The late flowering or show varieties are among the brightest ornaments of the garden. We regret so few of the many sorts are suitable for forcing, or for early flowering in the "window." The following varieties can be successfully grown in pots, giving them the same soil and treatment as recommended for the Hyacinth. They should be planted in five-inch pots, putting five bulbs in each, one in the centre, the four equally distant about one inch from the rim. Plant as early as they can be procured in the fall. Plunge out of doors, and let them remain until the first of December, when they may be brought in. As soon as they show signs of growth, water moderately; give them plenty of light, sun, and air; a cool situation suits them best.

Fig. 33.—Pot of Tulips.

Duc Van Thol, Red and Yellow—single; the earliest variety.
do do double; showy and early.
Scarlet—very bright and showy.
White—very fine, large, and perfect flower.
Yellow—one of the best yellow sorts grown.
Crimson—large flower, but not so early.
Gold striped—early, and very showy.
Potterbakker, White and Yellow—Both are good for forcing; flowers larger than the Duc Van Tholl's, but not as early; very fine for a succession.
Tournesol, (double), Red and Yellow—a very large flower, opens wide, is a free bloomer, and very showy.
Florentine (sweet scented)—exquisite on account of its delicious fragrance.

With these varieties we advise the amateur to stop, as we think the room can be filled with plants that are better adapted to indoor culture.

The Narcissus

Is admirably adapted for window gardening; soil and general treatment same as for the Hyacinth. They should be planted in September, one in a pot, which should be not less than five inches across. Place out of doors, where they should remain until near Christmas, by which time they will be well rooted, and ready for rapid growth. After flowering, they should be left in the pots, and kept growing until they can be plunged in the garden, where they should be left (in pots) for the next season. After they have become well established they flower profusely. But few kinds of bulbs are so impatient of changes as these; they should not be taken out of the pots until the bulbs and roots have completely filled them; then take out, remove the outside bulbs, leaving the centre in a solid mass, and repot for the next season. The shifting should be done when the bulbs are at rest. The following are the most desirable for indoor culture:

Polyanthus Narcissus, (Roman,) double; white and yellow; when planted early will bloom at Christmas.

Fig. 34.—Basket of Mixed Bulbs.

Paper white; pure white, and early; very fine.

Grand Soliel d'Or, fine yellow orange; cup very handsome; comes in after the preceding.

States General, lemon yellow; orange cup; an excellent variety.

Bezelman major, white; yellow cup; a later variety, but one of the very best.

Double Narcissus, Albo pleno oderato, very double; pure white; later than the Polyanthus Narcissus, and should be left out of doors until it has been frozen hard before bringing in; it will bloom about the first of March.

Single Narcissus, Porteus, a popular and well-known variety, pure white, lemon-colored cup in the centre, which is bordered with bright crimson.

Single Narcissus, Albo simplex oderato, pure white; very fragrant.

Jonquilles, large double and single; sweet scented; both very desirable for forcing.

In large collections, all the above varieties of Narcissus are desirable. The number of bulbs required will, of course, depend upon the space that can be spared for them. Like other kinds of bulbs, it is well to have a good supply in reserve, as they need not be in the conservatory or drawing-room more than three or four weeks; consequently, a large number will be required for from December until May, the season that the amateur's time is wholly taken up with the scores of favorites that now claim care and attention, out of doors.

Crocus.

The Crocus, which has for many ages been cultivated as an ornament to our flower gardens, can, if properly managed, be made an effective plant for the conservatory or ordinary house culture. The first thing of importance attending their culture is early planting, which should be attended to early in September. Few bulbs suffer more from being kept too long out of ground than these. The soil best adapted to them is a rich, light, sandy loam. Plant, for a good display, six to ten bulbs in a pot, colors to be arranged according to taste. A few small

Fig. 35.—Box of Bulbs growing in Sand.

pots, with but one color in each, contrasts better with other plants in the window than larger pots of mixed sorts. When planted, plunge the pots out of doors, same as Hyacinth, and let them remain until Christmas, when they may be brought in and given plenty of light and air, keeping cool until they begin to show bloom, when they may be placed in the window as wanted. With these precautions, a fine display can be had. A succession of bloom may be kept up by bringing in as wanted. Disappointment generally arises from keeping them

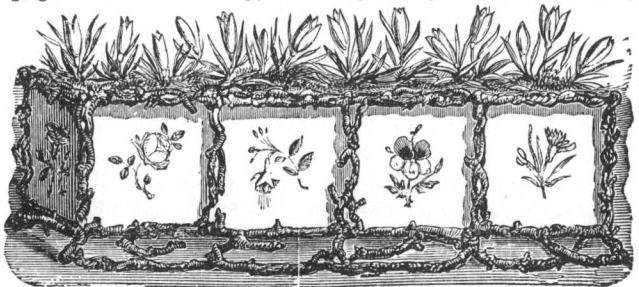

Fig. 36.—Tile Box filled with Bulbs.

too warm in the early stages of their growth. The following varieties are the best for pot culture, giving very large flowers of great substance, with rich and very beautiful colors:

Albion, very large white.
Albertine, white, striped violet
Charles Dickens, large purple.

David Rizzio, deep purple.
Florence Nightingale, large, fine white purple throat.
La Majesteuse, violet-striped, on a delicately tinted ground.
La Neige, snow white.
Mont Blanc, large, pure white; purple base.
Mammoth, very large, pure white.
New Golden Yellow—The bulbs of this variety are very large, each bulb producing from ten to fifteen flowers.
Queen Victoria, fine, pure white.
Sir Walter Scott, beautifully pencilled lilac, very large, and of great substance.
Lord Palmerston, sky blue; very pretty.
Cloth of Gold, golden yellow, striped brown; one of the earliest varieties.
Princess af Wales, very large, and fine, pure white.

After flowering, throw away, as they do not do well after, and the low price they are sold at enables a replenishment at less cost than the trouble of saving.

Bulbocodium, or Red Crocus,

Commonly known as Spring Colchicum, is a charming plant for pot culture, requiring the same treatment as the Crocus; flowers of purple red, which are produced in great numbers from a single bulb. They may be brought in about the middle of December, and will flower at Christmas. They require plenty of water during flowering, after which they should be slowly dried off until the leaves dry up; then lay away for next season's flowering.

The Snowdrop.

This ever popular and charming little flower, the first to welcome spring when planted in some snug corner where the sun loves to linger, is quite at home in the window-corner. It thrives finely in a light, sandy loam; does not require to be particularly rich. If planted in pots alone, six can be put in a three-inch pot, which should have the same treatment as the Crocus, a little freezing being very beneficial to them. They make a lovely border to the pots or boxes of Hyacinths, the same treatment answering equally well for both. The double is larger and better for pot culture than the single; the latter is the earlier of the two. It is of no use to plant these bulbs unless it is done in September, for they soon spoil from dry rot if left long out of ground. For house culture the better plan is to take from the open border where the bulbs have remained undisturbed a number of years. With these success is almost certain, while with newly imported bulbs failure is not uncommon.

The Winter Aconite,

Is a charming little plant, with golden blossoms, which expand simultaneously with the Snowdrop, and with which it contrasts finely. After flowering, the foliage makes a beautiful edging for pots or jardinets.

The Iris

But few plants present such rare beauty, and rich combination of color as the Iris. The name was given it by Pliny and Theophrastus, from the variety of its colors. Of the many hundred varieties, the bulbous rooted sorts are the only ones that succeed well in pots. The method of culture is simple, requiring a rich loamy soil. Only three or four bulbs should be planted in a six-inch pot, which should be filled about one quarter full with broken pots for drainage, then fill with soil, and press the bulb in so that the top of the bulb will be even with the rim of the pot. Give but very little water until they show growth; after which it may be given more freely.

The English Iris, for brilliancy of color and vigorous foliage, takes rank among the handsomest of flowering bulbs, they grow nearly two feet high, and produce during June and July, a succession of large and beautiful flowers. This variety is too large to become popular as a window plant.

The Spanish Iris, differ materially from the English, though no less beautiful; they are not as large as the former, and bloom somewhat earlier, which makes them more desirable for pot culture.

Iris Pavonia, or Peacock Iris, is a charming little plant well adapted for pots. The bulbs are quite small—not much larger than peas. They should be planted in September or October, in a light turfy loam. Plant three or four bulbs in a four-inch pot, which should be kept in a cold frame until toward Spring when they may be brought in and watered moderately; they will soon begin to make growth, and will flower early in April.

Iris Persica, is the best for forcing. Plant the same as I. Pavonia; they will flower almost as soon as brought in; the colors are white, blue, purple, and violet. They are highly prized for their delicious fragrance, which is fully equal to the violet. This sort will bloom in water like Hyacinth.

Iris Susiana, is one of those beauties that baffle description. It is one of the best for the "window," flowering freely in pots, jardinets or vases. It is the earliest sort, consequently the most desirable for winter decoration.

The Ixias, and sister cape bulbs the Sparaxis, Babianas and Tritonias, are amongst the most graceful, attractive and beautiful of cape flowering bulbs. Though differing considerably in style and habit of growth, they require the same cultural treatment. They succeed best in good turfy peat. Plant about the first of October, three or four in a four-inch pot, which should be placed in a cold frame, protected from severe frosts and heavy rains. They should be brought in about the first of March; they will at once commence growth and flower early in April.

The color of the Ixias are of every conceivable shade, forming some of the most remarkable contrasts. The habit of the plant is most graceful, and when a quantity are in bloom, the effect of it is most pleasing. In selecting these bulbs, choose named sorts, for the same reason you would many other bulbs, viz: bulbs in mixture are apt to be bulbs of the more common sorts.

Sparaxis, are more dwarf and compact in habit than the Ixia, while their colors are as varied and beautiful. For pot culture and window decoration they cannot be too strongly recommended.

The Tritonia, in habit and form, is very similar to the Sparaxis. They are plants of rare beauty, colors principally *selfs*. For good effect about twice as many bulbs should be put in a pot as of the Ixia.

The Babiana, in habit and growth, is nearly the same as the two former, but as unlike in color as is possible for such near relatives. While the others are mostly crimson and white, with their various shades, these are nearly all purple and blue. Together, they are most desirable, and are annually becoming more extensively used for window decoration.

Ranunculus.

This family is almost endless in variety, embracing some of the most common forage plants. While the Persian and Turban varieties produce the most elegant and diversified colored flowers, that for symmetry and compactness are unequaled. When properly grown they are completely covered with flowers nearly as large and quite as desirable as roses. But little attention has been given them as pot plants; our experience with them, as such, has been most pleasing, having had more truly handsome flowers than from almost any other plant, with the same amount of trouble and expense.

For winter flowering, if possible, select roots that have been kept out of ground the previous season as they come into flower much earlier than those taken up the previous summer. The roots keep well in a dry place for two years, so that a succession of bloom can be obtained by planting at proper intervals, the whole season.

The Ranunculus, requires a strong, fresh, loamy soil, made very rich by well rotted cow manure; with such components use equal parts. For early blooming, commence potting the first of August. Use four-inch pots, into which put three roots of separate colors, selection of which to suit the taste; place the roots firmly in the mould, and cover half an inch; plunge the pot or put in a shaded frame; bring in as wanted, commencing the first of October, give them a light warm situation, and shade from the sun which completely destroys their bright colors.

For flowering the whole season, pot from August to April, and forward as wanted. The Persian varieties are the earliest, consequently should be planted first, to be followed by the Turban varieties. These two are the only varieties desirable for pot culture; but there are hundreds of named sorts, to be selected from seedsmen's catalogues that generally list the most desirable kinds. After blooming they can be dried off gradually, put in a dry place and kept for next year's flowering. The low price they are sold at does not make it an object to keep them for flowering the second year, as roots grown in the open border are generally more satisfactory.

Anemone.

Of this plant there are nearly a hundred species, each with its score of varieties, many of them present some of the finest forms of floral beauty. The double varieties are the best suited for the conservatory, and for which they are admirably adapted; the foliage is extremely beautiful, the bright green contrasting well with the dazzling brightness of the bright scarlet and purple flowers that grow in profusion. They require the same general treatment as the Ranunculus, only that a little sea sand or salt should be mixed with the soil. For a succession of bloom, plant from September until March. Those planted in September will flower in latter part of March or the first of April, while those planted in March will flower by the middle of June.

We list the following from many we have bloomed, and should recommend them for pot culture.

Feu Surperbe, bright scarlet.
Rose Surpassante, rose.
Queen of the Netherlands, white and rose, fine.
L'Ornament de la Nature, rich dark blue.
Lord Nelson, violet.
Queen Victoria, bright scarlet, a free bloomer.
Rembrandt, carmine.
Shakspeare, beautiful blue.
Von Schiller, dark brilliant blue.

The above collection includes the most striking and positive colors, and are such as bloom well. Many others might be added to the list without materially increasing the value of the collection.

The Cyclamen.

About this flower but one opinion can be entertained,—that it is the most beautiful bulbous rooted plant ever introduced for the parlor or conservatory, and its beauty is fully equaled by its adaptation for the same purpose. We are fully justified in making this assertion, by the greatly increased interest taken in it by florists, amateurs, and the lovers of flowers in general. Ease of culture is an additional feature in their character and much in their favor. The difficulty in propagation alone has prevented their becoming a florists flower. The roots or bulbs of the Cyclamen being a solid corm, they will not divide successfully; consequently the only means of propagation is from seed, which must be gathered soon as ripe, slowly dried, and planted in a green house in heat; they must be kept constantly growing until they are in full flower. This part we should advise the amateur to leave to the professional florist and depend upon such for plants for the first season.

They should be procured soon as they show flower, place in a sunny exposure and not be allowed to get chilled in winter. They are generally offered for sale about Jan. 1st. If in a warm room, even temperature, and kept well watered they will remain in flower until the first of May; after flowering they should be plunged into a shady border, and left to care for themselves until there is danger of frost when they should be taken in, repotted in a compost of leaf mold, turfy loam and well rotted cow manure in equal parts; use pots in proportion to the size of the bulb. A pot twice the diameter of the bulb is plenty large; a pot six inches in diameter is sufficiently large for the largest bulbs. After repotting, water moderately until they commence growth, then apply as needed. We saw several bulbs last season that had not been shifted for several years; several of them gave over two hundred flowers each; more exquisite pot plants could not be had

Scilla,

Of various kinds, have long been popular as early spring flowers; S. Siberica is of the most intense blue, and is a perfect gem, whether in the open border, in pots or any device that is used for Hyacinths, Tulip or Crocus—it can be mixed with either of them with most excellent effect, requiring the same treatment. The habit of it is exceedingly dwarf, growing but little larger than the Crocus. The flowers are borne on a slender stalk, of bell-shape, similar to a minature Hyacinth. S. Amoena, is also very beautiful as a pot plant, being a little taller and later than the Siberica—it is very useful as a succession. There are several other varieties, very beautiful for out-door cultivation but not suitable for pots.

Muscari.

M. botryoides, the Grape Hyacinth, is remarkable for its dwarf growth and neat compact heads of bloom. The three varieties, dark blue, light blue and white, make charming clumps, when planted in pots two or three of a color in each. They require but little room, a six inch pot being sufficiently large for a dozen bulbs; the same soil and treatment recommended for the Hyacinths is best suited to them. After flowering they may be allowed to ripen off slowly and they will bloom equally well for a number of years. Muscari Plumosum or Feathered Hyacinth, does not thrive well in pots generally, but should be grown in small quantities. Their remarkable plume-like appearance, so unlike any other flower, is of sufficient importance to entitle them to a place in the conservatory. Treat same as the other varieties.

Amaryllis.

This splendid and beautiful family has not as yet received the care and attention, or become as generally cultivated as their rarity and excellence deserves, containing as it does so many varieties of surpassing loveliness, beauty and grandeur. These qualifications alone should insure them a place in every "Window" Garden. Yet they have other recommendations for extensive culture, namely, that they can be made to produce their gorgeous and magnificent flowers nearly every month in the year. They are on this account invaluable for the conservatory and drawing rooms, which can be kept gay by the many truly elegant varieties as we now possess nearly the whole winter. The length of time they keep in flower, and the very pleasing variety they make, is another just claim they have for a high place among decorative plants.

The Amaryllis delight in good, light turfy loam, with the addition of a little well rotted cow manure, when planted in large pots, and all the conditions of growth are favorable, they throw up magnificent spikes of bloom. A. Johnsoni has been known to flower twice a year, a single bulb throwing up at one time four spikes, each giving four flowers. A more splendid flower than this is, it is scarcely possible to conceive. We scarcely know how to advise the amateur in the manner of treatment, but will commence with the dry bulb, which should be potted in the above compost, say in a six inch pot, fill nearly to the rim and press the bulb firmly in; one-half its diameter should be above the surface; give it a thorough watering, and place on a shelf in moderate heat; it will not require further attention until it shows signs of growth, the time of which will depend wholly upon circumstances, *i. e.*, how long it has been dry, the time of year, and whether it has been properly cared for during its rest. As a general thing the first indication of growth will be the flower stalk, which makes almost a perceptible growth, at this period. Give water freely once a week; a sprinkling of liquid manure is very beneficial; give plenty of light and moderate heat and the first flowers will be perfected in two or three weeks; large well developed bulbs will commence to throw up the second flower stalks about the time the first flowers are opened, which will make the flowering of a single bulb last from five to six weeks.

After flowering they should be immediately repotted, no matter what time of year, and given plenty of heat and water. Fully exposed to the light, they will grow most luxuriantly and the bulbs will grow in a proportionate degree, laying up strength and nutritive matter that will produce in due season another crop of magnificent flowers. When the leaves naturally show symptoms of ripeness or decay, water should be gradually withheld, and when fairly decayed the pots should be placed in a dry, airy situation away from the frost or rain; here they may remain for two months, when they should be placed in a tub of water and left an hour, then placed in a warm room for flowering again. The method of culture, as recommended here, is only to be applied to those known as Heppeastrom, which, unlike the Vallota, Belladona and other varieties, are under the florist's control and can be made to flower the whole season. An enthusiast, whose ten by fifteen green house we delight to visit, grows large quantities of Amaryllis, Johnsoni and its varieties, and gets from each bulb two crops of flowers annually. He gives each two months for flowering, two for growth, and two for rest, which he considers the best treatment, and no one that has seen the spikes of bloom that he produces can question his theory.

Vallota Purpurea,

Is one of the finest Amaryllis, and is the most easily managed. They are not at all particular as to soil, will grow in any, but prefer the same as recommended for other Amaryllis But few plants answer as well or make as fine display for the window. Unlike most other plants, they do not require shifting but will grow from year to year in the same pot, tub or box without a change of soil, or other care than to give them plenty of water while flowering or in their growing state, and moderate watering the balance of the season. The foliage being persistent they require attention the whole year, but they can be kept under benches, in a light cellar or in any light room away from the frost during the winter, and in summer anywhere out of doors upon the piazza, the lawn, or if in pots, plunge in the border. They require but little pot room, in fact do better when root bound. The writer had a clump in a small tub last season that gave forty-one spikes of bloom; the plant was but five years from a single bulb. It is truly one of the finest, cheapest and most desirable cape bulbs.

Its season of flowering is August and September, and we have neither been able to coax or drive it into flower at any other season.

The Lily.

One of the finest flowers in every sense of the word, too well known to need description. Every one knows what a Lily is. Most every one knows how to grow it. Our only regret is that it is not better adapted for the window. All or nearly all the varieties can be grown in pots, as well as in the border. The only objection for the "Window" being the season of flowering, that is from July to September in the open border. Many kinds will not vary but a few days with any treatment we have tried. The following varities are an exception to the rule, and can be made to bloom early in April.

Lilium Candidum.

L. Candidum, or common garden Lily, more generally known than any other, and we think one of the finest. In fact, as much as we admire and love the whole family, could we have but one, it would be *this one;* can be forced for the conservatory better perhaps than any other. It must be potted in August, soon after flowering, while at rest. Here let us remark that while many other kinds can be moved at almost any season of the year, this one cannot, only when at rest, a period of not more than four weeks duration. There has been more disappointment in buying this than all others together, as orders given for it in spring will most likely be filled by seedsmen generally; and not one that has been kept out of ground during the winter will bloom the following summer. It generally takes two years, frequently three, before they can be made to flower, when, if taken up at the proper time and planted at once, they are certain to flower. The reason is simple enough; they make the bulb in fall that is to bloom in spring, and if they are not allowed that privilege they simply bide their time at the expense of the grower's good nature.

The bulbs should be placed in six inch pots, top of the bulb even with the rim of the pot. Soon as potted plunge in the border to save trouble. Bring in before heavy frosts and place on slight bottom heat; water freely; give plenty of light and air and they will come into flower by Easter. They will bloom with out bottom heat in the window by giving them a warm sunny situation, but do far better with it. The best soil for them is a light turfy loam, one-third well rotted cow manure. Fresh manure must not be used in any case without a crop of disappoinments is preferable to a crop of Lilies.

Liliun Longiflorum.

Another beautiful pure white Lily, succeeds well in pots, requiring the same soil and general treatment as the Candidum. The bulbs of this variety can be obtained from November until spring. For the window they should be potted early in November, and kept moderately wet and warm until they show sign of growth, when they can be put in position for blooming. As a house plant the habit of this makes it more desirable than most any other. It is very dwarf rarely growing more than fifteen inches high.

Liliun Auratum,

The praise of which would fill a volume as its fragrance would fill a house, is another sort that succeeds well in a pot, box or any other way in which it may be planted, if we except a highly enriched soil which would be fatal to it. It will come into flower about the first of May, with the same treatment as the foregoing.

We know of no other Lilies that are well adapted for the Window Garden, not having been successful in growing others in this way. For out of door culture we most heartily beg leave to introduce the whole family from the least to the greatest to all lovers of flowers.

The Tuberose.

It is nearly three hundred years since the Tuberose first flowered in Europe, having been sent from the West Indies, by Father Minuti, to one of the celebrated gardens near Toulon, about the year 1594. It is to day the same pure, modest, unassuming and deliciously fragrant flower it was then. It is one of those gems that no one would change if they could, or could if they would. It may be considered perfectly beautiful from the fact of its being the first sought after on all occasions, whether of joy or mourning. It is, too, one of the few flowers that can be had at all seasons of the year. The only difficulty being the selection of bulbs, which should in all cases be left to the experienced grower or responsible dealer, as not one-half the bulbs sold will produce flowers under any circumstances; not that it is difficult to grow good bulbs, but it is to properly cure and keep them ready for planting. Dry bulbs can be obtained at all times which are the ones for forcing or planting out. It is of but little use to take up bulbs that have grown in the garden during the summer for flowering in pots in the "Window." To be successful use five inch pots, fill with a mixture of loam and well rotted manure in equal parts, press the bulb in about one-half its length and place it in a hot bed, or plunge the pot on a bench of the green house where they can have a gentle bottom heat, which is a necessity for flowering. They very soon begin to grow and should be kept warm and watered freely. Soon as they throw up the flower stalk remove to the conservatory, when they will soon flower and remain in bloom for several weeks. Good bulbs should average twenty flowers to a spike. After flowering throw away, as the bulb only flowers once Stock is kept up by off-sets. Those who do not have the convenience of a green house or hot beds for starting the bulbs must do the next best. We have frequently started them on the mantel in the kitchen, by taking a box narrow and long enough to hold three or four pots, which are put in the box filled with ashes or tan which should be kept wet to better retain the heat. They will start very well in this way using wood ashes for mulch. A Bulb which we once had flowered in the pot and gave us forty-five large and perfect flowers. For an ordinary Window Garden, one or two pots at a time is quite sufficient. The

Fig. 37.—Glasses used as Bouquet Holders.

most convenient way and about as cheap a one as any, is to buy bulbs with flower stalks started from a florist. This is meant to apply to the large number that love flowers but do not like to work for them.

Achimenes.

These tuberous rooted plants, generally classed with bulbs, are charming for growing in pots, pans and hanging baskets, either in assorted or individual colors. The flowers combine great individual beauty with richness and brilliancy Much importance should be attached to the Achimenes from the ease in which they can be induced to flower in the winter. The best soil for growing them is a light rich loam. The tubers should be put singly in three inch pots and placed in as warm a situation as the conservatory affords. Where bottom heat can be given them they will do much better. A moist atmosphere, with the thermometer from 70 to 80 degrees at mid-day, are requisites for specimen plants After flowering, gradually withhold water, turn the pots on their sides, in a dry place where they can remain until wanted the following season. When at rest they should remain in the pots. If long exposed to the air the roots become worthless. By starting at intervals of three to four weeks a succession of bloom may be kept up the whole season.

Lily of the Valley.

Who does not know and admire this, the loveliest child of the floral family? Why it is not found in every garden, conservatory, "window," or greenhouse, it is difficult to imagine, for there is scarcely a plant more easily cultivated than this. It is easily forced into bloom, and may be kept in succession from Christmas until May. For winter or spring flowering, take from the border, clumps as large as will fill pot, box, or any device in which they are wanted to bloom, using a rich strong loam. After potting, plunge out of doors, where they will be sure to freeze hard. Any time after, they may be brought into the greenhouse or conservatory, where they should be given bottom heat, and kept at the highest possible temperature; 100° with a moist atmosphere, will very soon bring them into flower; a less heat will answer, but they will not come into flower as quickly. Light is by no means necessary, as they do quite as well on the floor, under the bench, or the pipes, as anywhere else. When once in flower place in any desirable situation. To maintain a succession a reserve should be kept in a cold frame or pot, and brought in as required. For small pots it is best to select only the strong crowns; place four to six in a pot three inches in diameter, and treat as above stated. After flowering, separate and plant in a strong rich soil, where they should remain undisturbed for two years, when they will be strong enough for forcing again.

Illustrations.

The Jardinets illustrated in Figs. 24 to 27—are constructed of pottery ware, filled with sand in the interior, with here and there an opening for the spike of flowers to grow from the bulb. Figs. 28, 30 and 31—are costly porcelain, intended as elegant mantel piece ornaments. The remaining illustrations are very simple, and need no special explanation.

CHAPTER XIV.

FERNERIES, WARDIAN CASES, AND FERN DECORATIONS.

The fern case offers to us the very simplest of all means of household plant pleasures. Many who cannot afford a green house, or conservatory, or go to the expense of fitting up a plant cabinet, will find an abundant solace in this simple and inexpensive method of growing indoor plants.

The use of these small glass cases for plants, are numerous. They occupy very

Fig. 38.—Fern, (Platyloma cordata.

little room, are usually ornamental enough to be placed on any table or parlor stand. When once filled, they need little or no attention for many weeks; require no unusual care as to watering; can be readily removed from one room to another; are not as quickly affected by changes of temperature as plants in the open air of our sitting rooms.

But a more favorable feature in their use is seen when we say that they afford the only successful means for obviating the effect of the dry heated air of our dwellings. They are reached by no dust, are free from the noxious exhalations

Fig. 39.—Interior of Fernery.

of coal fires or gas lights; and when a breath of cold air accidentally enters the room they are not chilled nor frosted if the thermometer in the room should chance to go below 35°. Their styles are so various and prices so reasonable, that any one can be suited at prices of from $3 to $25.

To any one living amid the anxieties of a troublesome parlor garden, which they cannot manage, there are but one or two satisfactory ways left for enjoyment. Either get a fern case, or be satisfied with a simple hanging basket.

The Wardian Case.

The history of the Wardian or fern case, dates back to 1829, when a gentleman by the name of Ward, of London, first noticed, accidentally, the growth of vegeta-

Fig. 40.—A Parlor Fernery

tion under a close glass. He had laid down the chrysalis of an insect with some mould within a glass bottle, and covered it over. A short time afterward, as he describes it, "a speck or two of vegetation appeared on the surface of the mould and, to his surprise, turned out to be a fern and a grass. His interest was awakened; he placed the bottle in a favorable situation, and found that the plants continued to grow and maintain a healthy appearance."

This was the first idea of the Wardian case. In 1842, Mr. Ward published his discovery relating to the "growth of plants in closely glazed cases," in a volume which contained the result of his experiments in raising plants, and also the way he made his discovery. In 1851, the Wardian case made its first successful appearance in public, at the "*Worlds Fair*," and from that time to this it has become more gradually known and better appreciated. Very few have yet

WINDOW GARDENING.

any knowledge of it, but it is one of the few things which in time will be as popular as flowers themselves are, and every window will be decorated with their presence.

It has been an invaluable means of introducing to the floral world, and successfully growing many most delicate plants from the tropics which otherwise would scarcely ever have been seen out of their native haunts. By its use the Botanist has been enabled to transport plants to and from great distances through extremes of climate; and yet so unfailing has been the working of it that cases judiciously planted have been known to maintain their freshness and vigor for nine years, and no air or water was ever supplied in that time.

It is quite curious to watch its operation, and to many it is evidently as much of an enigma as a pleasure.

Apparently, moisture is constantly being condensed and deposited on the glass sides of the case. This supplies the plants within, who give it out again, and yet none escapes; thus affording the spectacle of a little world by itself.

This moisture is very desirable for the growth of ferns, and in no other form can they be so successfully and evenly maintained as here; nor can any other variety of plants furnish so interesting a study.

The Lycopodiums are very suitable and grow very satisfactorily. They drop their pendant roots, and, under the influence of the moisture, spread rapidly along the surface of the earth in the case, and filling up the bare spots, make a velvety covering of light feathery green, thus inducing shade and moisture.

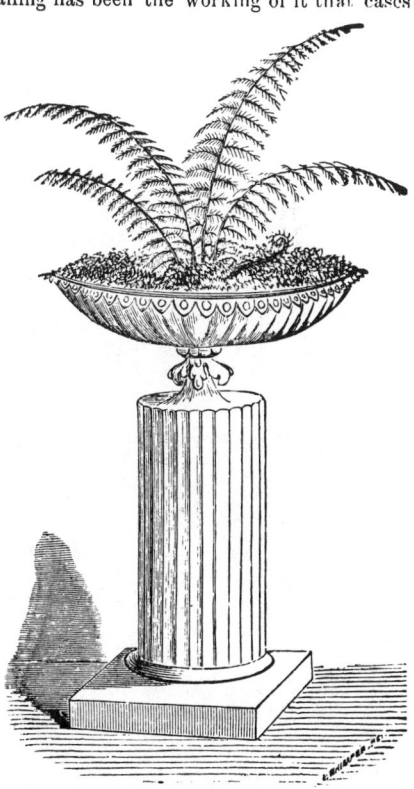

Fig. 41.—A Fern Vase.

Countless seedlings of ferns and lycopodiums will spring up, of the different varieties, and their unfolding fronds and subsequent development will be exceedingly interesting to you. You will be agreeably astonished and surprised when some fern, supposed by you to be dead, suddenly raises its head above the surface and shoots rapidly upward to let you see its vitality is not to be questioned.

As a pleasure, then, the Wardian case deserves a cordial reception; but it will be far more welcome to that class of our plant lovers who have often felt the disappointment in their pot plants, many of the best of which, notwithstanding the closest care, will show the yellow leaves and drop off, or the buds develop but an imperfect blossom ; the fern case will prove to be their refuge in distress, a never failing source of interest and amusement.

Principles of the Fern Case.

Let us understand the principles of fern cases and the operation and life of plants within. Those of you who have observed plants under bell glasses or

Fig 42.

shades, have noticed that the moisture often collects so quickly inside as to actually obstruct or prevent the plant from being seen, and have wondered where this moisture came from.

The answer to this question is simple : "*From the earth, the plants, by exhalation,* i. e. *vegetable perspiration.*" But you ask again : " *Why does it collect so largely ?*" and we reply : "Simply because we confine it, and prevent its escape and evaporation by making our case airtight. If the case were ventilated, its temperature would be moderated to correspond with the atmosphere of the sitting

WINDOW GARDENING. 163

room. And this is the very thing we do not want. Our case then should be made air tight, for the purpose of not only confining this moisture, but of keep

Fig. 43. A Large Fern Case

ing a constant and abundant supply of it, for the plants must have a congenial atmosphere of their own and cannot live without the proper moisture.

You cannot expect your ferns or plants to grow nicely in this moist atmosphere if you open the case every few days: It has the same effect as change of climate, or open air exposure to a sick person accustomed only to the air of the house. The confinement of ferns in these close cases has the tendency to make them delicate, and the sudden opening of the case, with the introduction of the hot, dry, dusty air from the rooms, is against all reason.

Fig. 44.—A Fern Window and Aquarium.

It is sufficient to say, therefore, that when once planted and closed, the fern case needs no ventilation. Let it live by itself.

Drainage.

This point comes up for discussion, and the only answer we give is to ask another question : " Do plants need drainage when the water is being constantly evaporated and thrown off in the open space above the plants ?" In other words, the plants are draining themselves constantly. Here is one great advantage of the fern case over the pot plant, the latter requires constant watering, the former none at all, for no water escapes. Then a fern case may be handled with impunity by one in whose hands we would not trust a row of pot plants, and so is beyond the reach of the careless or forgetful.

Management.

Whether your case is of wood, glass, or metal, you will require a pan in which to hold the plants. Zinc pans answer every purpose, combining economy and durability. Tin should not be used as it will soon rust and wear out.

No pan should be less than four inches deep, unless the plants are very dwarf specimens, and then an inch less in depth will do, though there might be some risk of crowding the roots too much. Then, again, too great a depth is objectionable. The best rule to observe is as follows : Ferns, whose fronds are not over eight inches in length, should be planted in a pan four inches in depth. Larger ferns may require a pan five to six inches in depth, but four inches will generally be found sufficient for all purposes.

Those who try the shallow and deep pans will soon find how much more freely their plants grow when plenty of space is allowed for their roots. A side opening to the glass case is to be preferred in all cases, whether by hinged doors or sliding panes. This avoids reaching in at the top of the fern case, which, besides being extremely awkward, often results in the breaking of the fronds or the leaves.

The *height of the case* is an important point. Under glass, a plant or fern, will often develop a greater length of frond, than under any different circumstances. Make your cases high, so that all fronds may have room to develop and expand to full size ; and the height should not be less than twice the diameter. In cramped quarters, and cases chosen perhaps too small, filled with too robust plants, their growth is often summarily checked by reaching the top of the glass ; there the fronds with no chance to get higher, lie flattened out against the surface of the glass collecting an undue amount of moisture, which soon causes it to mould or damp off. It becomes unsightly, and the beauty of many rare and fine looking specimens is endangered.

The forms and construction of fern cases will differ with the tastes of each individual. We do not recommend attempts at "home made" cases, on the side of mere economy, for there are now cases already prepared for use, at so cheap prices, and obtainable at proper places, that it is a waste of time to make one yourself. Very desirable cases are now imported, constructed of bases of pottery, with dishes all complete, and the glass shade ready to fit upon the top—only wanting the soil and the plants from the florist. Very good cases are also made of wood bases, and the cost for either will not exceed $3 for circular cases 12 inches in diameter, to $6 or $10 for 18 inches to 2 ft. in diameter.

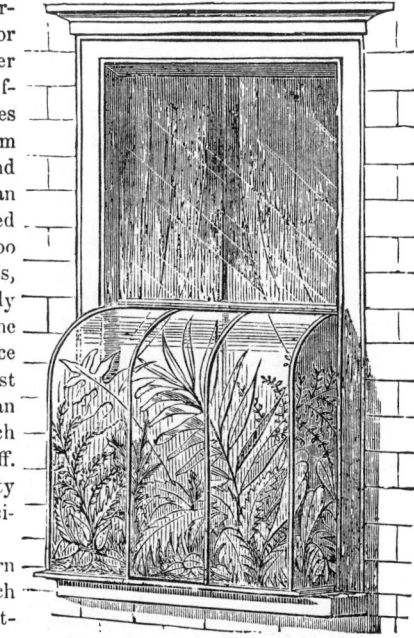

Fig. 45.—Ferns in a Window Garden.

The larger your case, the better, provided it is not too bulky. It should be in form easily handled, light in weight ; and if square, or in any other form than round, should have a small door to reach the plants without lifting the glass top. *The soil for fern cases*, should be carefully attended to; no common garden earth will answer; get it from the most reliable florist if possible,—and even some of these may not know exactly the needs of the plant. For ferns, choose leaf mould one part, silver sand one part, dry friable peat two parts. Avoid that peat which comes from wet unhealthy situations. Wherever you see ferns growing near the edge of woods or running streams, you can be safe in taking some of the same soil, if you cannot get a good compost anywhere else. English florists, who have access to special materials, make up a particular compost of the fol

Fig. 46.—Heated Fern Case.

lowing materials which is described as perfect. Mix equal parts of silver sand good loam, powdered charcoal, refuse of cocoanut fibre. If you wish, you may cover the bottom of the pan with a layer of powdered charcoal, or bricks or gravel broken to the size of hazel nuts, to a depth of one inch, if pan is four inches deep; or one and one-half inches if 6 inches deep. Do not take the advice of those who recommend filling the pan half full with small charcoal; such a proportion is unnecessary. When the soil has been placed in the pan press firmly that all the plants may be set solidly.

Location for fern cases. They will do well *anywhere*, and that is just what the

Fig. 47.—Fern Case.

168 WINDOW GARDENING

amateur wants. They may be shifted from one window to another at pleasure, with little fear of dangerous consequences. If placed in the south window keep them back a little from the heat of the midday sun. A half shady position is much better than a sunny one. A northern out look will suit them admirably if not too cold,—and an eastern or western one is at all times suitable.

It would be best to have tables provided especially for the fern case to rest upon. This should be strong and yet easily moved by castors, (use the brass ones, not the rubber or wooden ones.)

Fig. 48.—Fern Pillar.

If the cases are quite small, say within 9 inches diameter, they may be suspended, and some of these hanging ferneries are quite ornamental.

The secret of good management is told in a few words, viz., *water well after planting,* then shut up your case, and leave it to itself.

A successful fern case grower, writes us that " the most successful winter I ever had with ferns, was one in which I only watered the case once after planting, and only opened it a few times in the seven months from November 1st to June 1st—and then to remove dead fronds."

If you water sufficiently at time of planting, (and you need not water any more than ordinarily for pot plants,) you will have no occasion to water again. The closed case prevents all evaporation.

Some fronds of course will die or turn brown. These must of course be removed. Insects may invade your little plant home, and these must be removed, but there will not be many and they are easily disposed of.

Some of our florists recommend ventilation for the case, feeling that the plants will be much the better for the pure air and the sunlight. This may be done only when the temperature of the outer and inner air is about the same, and only for a short time. It should not be done frequently, but may be tried at long intervals of one or two months.

Avoid too much moisture. If there should be too much inside the case, open it daily until a little has evaporated into the outer air, and then close again. It will not need watering or opening again for a month or more.

Plants for The Fern Case.

In arranging your plants place the strongest growers in the centre, and the smaller at the sides.

Besides standard plants in the fernery, there are often introduced little hanging plants suspended from the top of the glass frame. Plants for this purpose are simply taken out of their pots, their balls of earth are surrounded with moss, tied with copper wire, a loop running from which is fastened into a hook in the top, and then it becomes a miniature hanging basket. In England small pots of gutta percha are manufactured for this express purpose.

You will perhaps be advised by some florists not to choose for your fern case any of our native plants, because it is difficult to transplant them from their native soil, just at close of summer when they have done growing, and compel them to continue life continuously thereafter, in opposition to their nature, which demands rest during the winter season. Nevertheless it is done, and many a pretty fern case is indebted to some plant treasure of this character stolen from Sylva's bowery retreats, to grace the setting room; they still thrive, despite the prognostications of wise heads as to failure.

Fig. 49.—Parlor Fern Stand covered with Glass.

The *Lygodium palmatum*, or Climbing Fern, is very suitable, and can be usually found in shady or moist spots in any of our Eastern States. It has a slender running root and stalk, from which proceed twining flexible stems, with very smooth palmate leaves or frondlets; these running stems or stalks are often three feet long, and the whole plant resembles in growth a delicate little Ivy. Besides its suitableness for the Fern Case, it is especially desirable for Rock Work in a conservatory.

The *Partridge Vine*, (Mitchella,) is also invaluable, for its brilliant scarlet berries enliven the sober green of the ferns or form an excellent contrast with the mosses. Take up large vines of it, with as many berries as you can procure;

if they are green when found, they will turn red very shortly; for covering soil and otherwise, naked or exposed, it is excellent.

The *Trailing Arbutus* (Epigœa repens) usually forms its buds in October or November, and blooms with full flower by January. These flowers are highly prized for their delicious fragrance, and it may be considered one of the choicest for our selection.

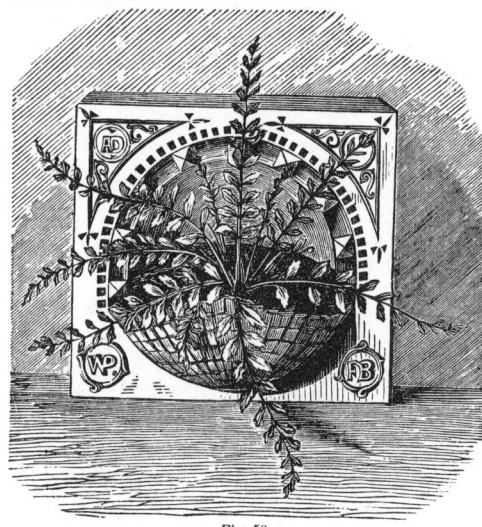

Fig. 50.

The *Maidens' Hair Fern* (Asplenium) is the first favorite for the Fern Case, the loveliest of our native ferns. It may be found on some sheltered hill side, or away in some deep, moist woods, known by its black, hair like stems, and curiously shaped fronds. Gather some of the very smallest specimens, and let them grow; take them up roots and all. When you gather up the roots take up also soil enough to fill your zinc tray or box. It will stand transplanting better if its proper soil is carried with it. It will not be amiss to take home an abundance for other purposes, to fill in the pots for Fuchsias, Roses and Carnations, which grow in your windows. Among other plants which you can transplant from the woods, are

The *Gaultheria procumbens*, or Wintergreen.
Chimaphilla, or *Pipsinima*, various species.
Pryola, or *False Wintergreen*, various species.
Sarracenia purpurea, or Side Saddle flower; their cups must be kept full of water.
Cypripedium, or *Lady Slipper*, or *Maccaron Flower*.
Speranthes, or *Lady Tresses*, various species.
Dionaea muscipula, or Venus' Fly Trap.

The *American Lycopodiums*, or Club Mosses, are all very desirable. Many of them are used freely for decorations at Christmas. The best varieties are *denticulatum*, *Wildenovii*, *umbrosa*, *dendroideum*, *lucidulum*.

The daintily cut foliage of the Captis trifoliata or Gold Thread, will form a pretty feature, and the Linewood, or *Hepatica*, with its blue eyes, will be no less lovely. The Wild Lily of the Valley (*Convallaria*) will open its tiny white bells long before they open in the meadow or at the brookside.

If you look for other mosses, larger than the *Lycopodium*, you can take the *Polystichum*, or Hair Cup moss; *Patraphis*, or four toothed moss; *Splachnum*, or Umbrella moss. You will need plenty of these green mosses or white lichens or the Sealing Wax moss, to pack about the roots of your plants, and help keep up a cool, wild, woody home-like retreat. The following are the most generally preferred Ferns:

Polypodium, various species.
Struthiopteris, Ostrich Fern.

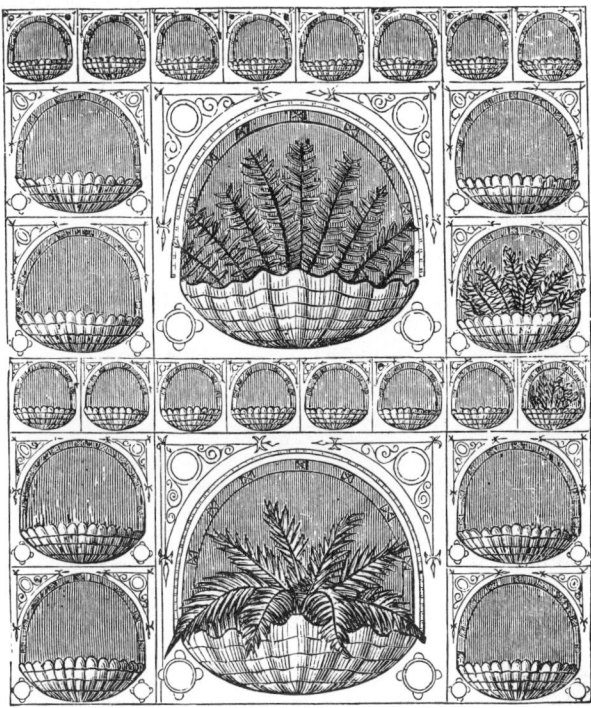

Fig. 51.—Group of Fern Shells.

Pteris, or Brocken.
Adiantum, or Maiden Hair.
Cheilanthes, or Lip Fern.
Woodwardia.
Camptosaurum, or Walking Fern.
Asplenium, or Spleenwood.
Dicksonia.
Cystopteris, or Bladder Fern.

Woodsia.
Polystichum, or Shield Fern.
Onoclea, or Sensitive.
Davallia Canariensis, or Hairs Foot Fern.

If your fern case is large enough you may add one or two large plants, such as the *Dracaena terminalis,* or *Nobilis;* the *Dieffenbachia variegata,* is very showy. The *Pandanus* or *Ananassa* may be admitted, and if you have plenty of room, there is no objection to the Crotons with their handsomely variegated foliage, the *Cissus discolor,* with blood red leaves and half trailing habit, the variegated leaved *Begonias,* also the *Gesnerias, Caladium, Colocasias, Marantas, Cacti, Saxifragas, Sedum.*

Fig. 52.—Ornamental Fern Case and Stand.

Avoid complication or crowding. If your case is of but moderate size, say two feet in diameter, use only one or two large upright plants; but if smaller than this stick only to the ferns and mosses.

Among other additional plants are:

The (*Goodyera pubescens*) Rattlesnake Plaintain; leaves variegated, dark green, with white veins.

The (*Erythronium*) Dogs' Tooth Violet, whose leaves are green mottled with brown.

For trailing purposes perhaps nothing is better than the *Lysimachia,* or Moneywort, and the Coliseum Ivy. *Orchids* may be added, if there is plenty of room, and nothing will give more satisfaction.

Do not expose those ferns with variegated foliage to severe sunlight, as they will suffer injury. Neither should delicate ferns be watered on the leaves. Some whose leaves appear but mere powder or dust, such as the Golden or Silver Fern, will lose their beauty if thus treated, and perhaps may be killed outright.

Exotic, or Green House Ferns.

Should you have ill success with your native plants and be undecided what to do we think it best for you to fall back upon something more suitable, and begin in a more simple manner, by going to the nearest green house, where ferns are grown, and procure some small seedlings. These come up in great quantities in the pots, also on the earth of the pan on which the pots rest, and in fact everywhere that the spores chance to sow themselves. You can in this way frequently get a half dozen varieties of ferns. Among them probably one or two *Adiantums*, a *Doodia*, and several varieties of *Pteris*. These are the ferns most likely to produce seedlings, when the spores are scattered over a moist surface.

After these have been transferred to the fern case, their daily growth will afford you a very pleasant and interesting study; the gradual change and growth of the frond from the first appearance to the full development will amply repay you for your patience in waiting.

This is the true way to enjoy plant cases; begin with the rudiments and learn step by step the nature of the plants.

For moderate sized cases we must select ferns of size and habit suitable for them.

The best of those found in green houses are: *Adiantum capillus Veneris, A assimile, A acristatum, Doodia aspera, D. caudata, Pteris geraniefolia, P. Cretica, albo lineata, P. heterophylla, P. serrulata, Blechnum gracile, Asplenium auritum*, and *A. bulbiferum*. There are many others, but a simple list like this is sufficient.

For tall ferns choose *Polypodium Aureum, P appendiculatum, Pteris argyrea, Asplenium Brasiliense, Adiantum macrophyllum, Anemia Phylitidis*.

In planting your ferns do not crowd them together, but give room for the full development of the fronds; their growth is rapid and many soon double their original size when first purchased. Alternate the different varieties if possible, and do not get two or three plants of the same kind together. A fine delicate fern always looks more graceful and pretty beside a variety with a full broad frond. So a light green or variegated plant will show to better advantage beside one with a dark green frond. In choosing your soil, make say of three parts rich, black peaty mould, one part coarse sand and gravel siftings mixed, and one part broken charcoal, see that the pieces of charcoal are broken to the size of cranberries, and well mixed with the earth; the whole should only be broken up, not sifted.

Fig. 53.—Parlor Fern Stand.

After you have put the plants in the case, water with a small watering pot with a fine nose. Saturate the earth pretty thoroughly, but not to make it muddy. There are many other varieties of the *Lygodiums* not mentioned above *Lygodium, apodum, densum, caesium, arboreum, lipidophyllum,* their roots will extend over the earth, covering all the bare spots with a fresh green carpet of delicate growth.

Should we be able to procure a plant of the greenhouse species of climbing fern, *Lygodium flexuosum,* or *L. japonicum,* another beautiful object will be added

Among the climbing ferns, are some of the most graceful ferns in the whole family of *Filices*. There is one plant, however, not a fern, which does exceedingly well in a fern case, and is remarkably interesting. We refer to *Ficus stipulata*. This plant, a vine, is a free grower, and climbs up the sides of our case by its roots, which, aided by the moisture on the glass, spread and adhere to it

Fig. 54.—Plant Case.

It is a hard wooded plant, roots quickly from cuttings, and grows so freely as to fill a moderate sized case very rapidly.

After you have become accustomed to growing ferns in the case, you will perhaps crave a little variety. This can be easily had. Suppose you look a little into the curiosities of growth and reproduction.

If you look on the under side of the fern fronds, you will find something resembling a brown powder, adhering to them thickly in regularly distributed masses of varied shapes, depending upon the species.

Examining with the magnifier or microscope, you find them to be seeds or spores.

Shake these spores, which appear like the veriest dust, over the surface of the earth in an ordinary fern case, after it has been well smoothened. The earth should be watered very thoroughly previous to scattering the spores

In about a month or six weeks, looking carefully across the surface of the earth, you see the slightest specks of green; again examining with the microscope you find them living organisms of vegetation ; and when at a later date they become of good size, it is with no little satisfaction to be able to say, that they were the seedlings sown by your own hand. If in your travels in the woods, you carry an herbarium with you, you can gather the fronds of every variety you meet, which contains fertile spores.

Spores from such an herbarium should be planted as soon as convenient to insure germination. Spores have been known to germinate as long as eighteen months after being gathered, while under favorable circumstances germination in spores has taken place, when sown eight or ten years after they were collected. From your spores you will get a quantity of seedlings, many of them of strange forms, and some to differ from the parent plant.

Fig. 55.—Arborette.

We may find frequently several fronds on the same plant differing very materially. Thus your love and knowledge of plant life increases, and you willl cherish your fern case with more than customary pleasure, for it opens up a new world to you.

One thing only remember *i. e.*, keep out of your fern case all the common bedding plants, such as Geraniums, Petunias, Verbenas, Roses, Fuschias, &c., for they cannot well stand the confined moist air.

Designs for Fern Decorations.

A home made plant case can be constructed as follows: Get your carpenter or cabinet maker to construct a shallow box, of fine wood, say black walnut, about two feet wide, and three or three and one-half feet long. The bottom board should be about an inch and a half thick, and project about an inch beyond the sides. The sides should be of inch stuff, and the depth six or seven inches. See that the corners are well dovetailed together, and on the inside of the tops cut a groove, into which to set the glass.

The size of your glass should be about two feet square for the ends, and two feet by thirty-six inches for the sides and top; but if this is too large and expensive a case, you can construct one of but half these dimensions, viz., twelve inches square for the ends and twelve by eighteen inches for the sides and top. Many like to have their cases made for them with pitched roof, like design No

Fig. 56.—Ferns in Arborette.

40, and with wooden frames same as for windows. All that it needs is to fit tne glasses into the frames and seal the sides up tightly with putty.

The frame, as it sets into the lower wooden box, should also be fastened well with putty, to make it tight; and on the outside you may fasten a very pretty little moulding, which will cover the top of the wood, and set snugly up to the glass. You will of course take care to have a little door cut in the back glass, say about six inches by eight or ten, opening or sliding, whenever necessary to introduce water, or remove insects and dead leaves.

Fig. 57.—Arborette.

In Fig. 42, the upper pane may be made movable

Next you will need a tray to go inside the wooden frame work. This should be of nearly the same size as the box, but smaller so as to fit inside. This tray should be constructed of zinc, and may be made with a double bottom of an inch in height, a small hole being cut in the upper one, for the purpose of carrying off any surplus water. The filling and planting have already been described. Place some broken charcoal, or fine brick or gravel, in the bottom of the upper pan, and then your compost over this. If your wood is well moulded, and sides ornamented, the case will be a very handsome ornament. Cases such as we describe, are now made and sold at prices of from $20 to $30, by all our large floral warehouses.

Fig. 58.—Arborette.

Should you wish to construct a little rockery in the fernery, select pieces of stone, sharp pointed, or with rough jagged sides. You will often find them in some moist spot in the woods, already half covered with moss; then build them up one above the other until you have made the form of an arch. Start the stones from the very bottom of the tray, mix the soil well with them wherever possible, into all the interstices, and if it is necessary to get cement to make them firm, do so. Then set set your ferns in all the rugged interstices of the stones, wherever you have placed the earth, and they will soon cover it with their leaves, and their roots will reach into all the crevices.

Design No. 40, is about the size we have described, constructed in a more than usually ornamental style. It is very suitable for all kinds of ferns, and *Lycopodiums, Small Orchids*, small species of the *Dracaena, Croton pictum, Cr variegatum, Aphelandra Leopoldi, Gymmostachys, Ver shaffeltii, Eranthemum, ifineum, Passiflora trifasciata, Alocassia, Caladium*, and *Fittonia argentea*.

Fig. 41 shows one of the simplest of all fern decorations in the form of a neat

WINDOW GARDENING.

vase; the bowl is filled with the proper soil, and its surface is covered with moss. In the centre is a nicely shaped plant of the *Maiden Hair Fern*, whose appearance gives a delightfully cool and refreshing feeling in the room. A very pretty effect could be produced by inserting little tubes of glass or tin (such as are used for holding cut flowers,) in the soil here and there among the moss, then filling with water and inserting at intervals clipped blossoms of some of your winter blooming flowers, Geraniums, Roses, Fuchsias, &c., or perhaps a clipped blossom from your climbing vines. Arranged any way it is in fact a beautiful object for the drawing room or conservatory.

In Fig. 39, is shown a most charming fernery, the property of Mrs. Shirley Hibberd, at Stoke Newington, London, England. This conservatory was located where sunshine was excluded on account of neighboring buildings and large trees, and a fern house was constructed. Rockeries were built up on two sides of the house, and in the crevices were planted ferns and lycopodiums. The floor was covered with neat tiles, and with the naturally graceful character of the plant the conservatory was peculiarly ornamented. The rockeries were made almost entirely of big blocks of peat, and on the top near the glass were planted a few Sedums, Sempervivums, and other succulent plants. Mr. Hibberd, in his description of the fernery, in his volume "Rustic Adornments for Homes of Taste," states that for the past twelve years about a hundred and fifty species and varieties have thriven here making summer all the year round in their perennial greenness.

Fig. 59.

The finest selections of ferns, as recommended by him for such a house, are the *Adiantums, Asplenium, Adiantum nigrum, Athyrium, f. f., A. f. f. crispa, Gymnogramma leptophylla, Doodias, Scolopendriums, Woodwardia radicans, Equisetum, Sylvaticum,* and *Selaginellas.*

Water was given daily during the warm weather; in spring and autumn, twice a week was sufficient, and in winter once in two or three weeks The plants must, however, never be left to get dry.

Miss Maling, an English lady writer on indoor plants, has invented a case (Fig. 42) which contains room for a hot water apparatus in the zinc pan. Her principle is to supply a cool or a heated end in the fern case, according to the necessities of the plants. "Hardy or greenhouse plants last long in flower at one end in the cool temperature; stove plants and forced flowers come on beautifully in the heated part. If all your plants in the case are hardy, then use no heat. If our ferns or flowers, though not wanting heat specially, should damp off; we give heat just for a time to change the air entirely. At ten minutes notice the

Fig. 60.

heat can be raised to any degree up to 90°. The cases are of two sizes, the larger ones being about four feet long, by two wide, and two high, while the boxes on which the glassed frames rest are eight inches deep. The boxes are lined with zinc, and fitted with hot water apparatus. No lamp or any heater is required, hot water only being used, which is poured in through a concealed opening from without, and when cold is let off by another opening.

Fig. 61.

This water maintains the temperature at a height sufficient for most plants for twenty-four hours without refilling; but when greater heat is required it can be raised to any degree from 65° to 90°, by adding more hot water after the first twelve hours. The upper glass sash is movable, and by a button or hook is lifted at any time ventilation is needed or you wish to examine the plants. This principle of heating the case is principally for the sake of bringing into flower and keeping in good health many tender stove plants, as well as other delicate plants which cannot stand either a cool or a dry atmosphere."

The general outline and construction of Miss Maling's plant case is very similar to the "home made case" we have previously described. Heating will be unnecessary if amateurs will only choose but the ordinary native or greenhouse ferns, and keep the case well closed away from cold air.

Fig. 62.

But it seems to us if the case is to be heated at all, it should be divided into two apartments, one end for plants needing the warm temperature, the other for the cool temperature, or else put no plants in the case unless they are all to be treated alike.

Whenever, in the mind of a beginner, there appears to be a doubt as to what to choose, take the *Lycopodium denticulatum*, and other varieties of *L. caesium, apodum, heloctica,* or *variabilis* will always appear to advantage; also the *Pteris cretica albo lineata,* or *Cyrtomium falcatum*, do remarkably well, being very strong growers."

These Fern Pillars are also made of Terra Cotta, in England, with openings in appropriate places for setting in the bricks. The columns are also constructed so as to permit a glass screen to shut completely over them and rest upon the base, thus giving the same effect as a Wardian Case. Fig. 49 shows another design on a table, with a glass top also. Fig. 50 shows one of the largest styles of fern bricks, as it rests fitted into a fire screen.

Fig. 51 is much more elaborate, and shows what may be done either in the side of a wall or a conservatory, or to occupy a large fire place. These are made in the form of square pieces of pottery, which may be nailed flat against the wall. In the lower portion of the front appears a projection of a shell, and within it is a small cavity for holding the plants. Being of various sizes, any style of arrangement can be ingeniously formed, and at slight expense.

These designs are as yet unknown in the United States, but can be quickly imported to order by any one; or our pottery manufacturers could soon supply any demand by making any pattern and casting therefrom.

They are elegant in appearance and effect, and the general testimony is to the effect that the ferns thrive very well in them.

Fig. 63.—Fern Stand.

Fig. 64.—Fern Stand.

Figs. 52 and 53 introduce several pretty Parlor Ferneries, of easy manufacture, the former in the shape of a rectangle, about 2 feet long by one and a quarter foot wide, and two feet in height. The other with six sides, curving to the top, from which suspends a little wire hanging basket. These designs are soon constructed by any cabinet maker.

A pleasant story is told of a gardener near London, England, who, instead of following the invariable fashion of devoting the high stone walls surrounding his enclosed garden, to wall fruit, determined to cover it with ferns.

"The wall was 14 feet in height and 400 feet in length. It was then very old, and having been originally built of a dark red brick, much in use in that day in the district, it had a venerable and picturesque appearance. From the ground line to the summit it was all the summer long dotted over with ferny tufts of herbage, some sparkling with the hue of emerald, others shading off to rich shades of brown and orange; and the delicate tracery of those with finely divided fronds, wonderfully set off like vegetable lace against the dark back ground of the weather-worn brick.

Fig. 65.

Nail holes had been made here and there, where in former times were fastened the branches of peach, apricot, cherry, and plum trees to ripen their crops; but they had long ago been given up. The idea occurred to him to convert it into a perpendicular fernery. He first of all thrust into some of the large holes in the wall, tufts of common *Polypody*, making their creeping roots comfortable with turfy peat, and securing them from falling out by means of a copper wire passed across the hole and held to the bricks by small staples. As these were found to flourish and give the wall somewhat the aspect of a ruin, he began to make holes to plant others; and by degrees the wall was covered with Hearts Tongue, *Asplenium adiantum*, the Wall rue fern, the Mountain Polypody, the *Alpine cystopteris*, and dozens of others that bear drought patiently, and naturally inhabit rocks and waysides. In the shady chinks next the butteries, he managed to coax the *Maiden hair* to make luxuriant fillets of herbage, and at the foot of the wall there were tufts of *lastrea, osmunda royal*, and other ferns which the wall itself refused to nourish The majority of these held their verdure far into the winter, the Hearts Tongue and common Polypodium were usually quite green the whole year round; and during the winter their rich dottings of golden spores sparkled in the most cheerful manner against the dark back ground of sheets of ivy and red brick. Of course the wall itself was crowned with *Snapdragons, Wallflowers,* and other gay tenants of ruined towers, or pines, that make riot of man's work, and glorify the decay of art with the triumph of nature."

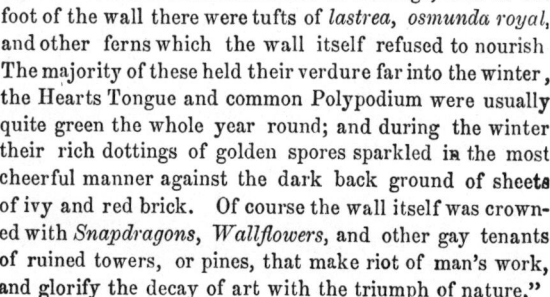

Fig. 66.

Figs. 55, 56, 57, 58, introduce several "*Rustic Terra Cotta Arborettes.*" These are made of Terra Cotta, or pottery ware, cast in a rugged form resembling the projecting limbs of an oak tree just clipped, and with cavities opening downward for the reception of earth and holding plants. Some of them have a solid interior, and each basin is by itself. These are undesirable, having no opportunity for drainage; but where the interior is entirely hollow and can be entirely filled with earth, no rustic ornament is more suitable for ferns or other plants to live in. They may decorate the hall, parlor, conservatory, or out door lawn. Their size is from one to three feet high

WINDOW GARDENING.

The strongest growing ferns may be placed in here, taking care to put a few crocks of broken brick or charcoal in the bottom of each basin for drainage.

They may be used also for spring flowering Bulbs, and filled with hyacinths, crocuses, scillas, snowdrops, narcissus; and then when these are over, the contents may be emptied and refilled again with summer flowering plants; but it is usually best to devote them to such classes of plants as will flower the year round without any change.

Figs. 59 to 66 show the different styles of mounting Fern cases with the customary cylindrical glass shades.

In Fig. 43, we see one of the larger styles of Miss Maling's designs, intended to set upon a table. This is most charmingly filled; and perhaps we cannot do better than let Shirley Hibberd himself, who filled it, tell us what is in it:

"It fell to my lot to construct the mimic archway (a rockery,) and fill it with pockets for the reception of small ferns. For that purpose I took two square seed pans, and placed them bottom upwards, on the zinc bottom of the case, as abutments, which, of course when the case was filled with soil, were hidden from view. From the flat foundation of clay thus provided, I began to build, using small pieces of coke dipped in a batter of cement, and spending a few hours every day for four days in succession upon the work ere it was completed. In the pockets were inserted specimens of *Cystopteris regia, Camptosaurus rhizophyllus, Asplenium flabellifolium, Scolopendrium, vulgare var ramosum, polyschides,* and *vulgare ramo marginatum, Adiantum hispidulum,* and a few *Selaginellas.* The latter soon grew so as to smother the whole fabric, forming a rich bell of various tints of blue and green, with the fern pushing through them. On the right hand side of the arch was planted *Nephrolepis exaltata,* one of the most suberb of Wardian Case ferns, and remarkably distinct, with its graceful arching polypodium-like fronds.

Fig. 67.—Fern or Flower Case.

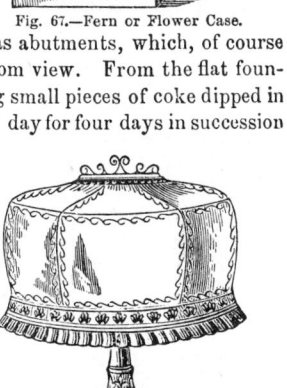

Fig. 68.—Case for preserving flowers fresh.

On the left hand *Nephrolepis pectinata,* which is of the same habit of growth, and a very beautiful and interesting fern; nevertheless, less beautiful than the other, as it is also less vigorous. A small plant of *Platycerium grande* was then planted in the shell of a cocoanut, and suspended by copper wire to the crown of the arch, and this spring its new growth was so vigorous that it had to be removed to the greenhouse, where it is now flourishing. Two more notable ferns were introduced, namely : *Pteris flabellata, var. crispa*, a very erect and characteristic fern of large growth, quite cheap and common, and one of the best for glass cases, of at least two feet in height within. The other was our fine old hardy friend, *Cyrtomium falcatum*, which is worth a place anywhere among ferns, and fortunately it will grow anywhere, and is always noble.

The rest of the plants consisted of various small, yet choice subjects. *Pteris scaberula*, very beautiful in the lace-like divisions, and light green hue of its fronds. It is really a gem, and always grows well in peat, cocoanut, or any soil of a light spongy texture.

Doodia lunulata and *caudata*, are of small growth, and serve well with *Lomaria lanceolata* and *L. spicant*, to fill up green tufts between ferns—of very distinct and striking appearance. In the centre of the case, but on the side opposite to the view here given, and hence hidden by the *Platycerium*—a plant of *Phlebodium sporodocarpum*—made a fine effect. It is one of the most distinct and beautiful and easily managed of all Wardian Case ferns, but must have always a nice peaty mixture.

Fig. 69.—Ladies' Plant Case.

The remaining ferns are *Polypodium phegopteris* and *rugulosum, Campyloneurum phyllitidis, Adiantum formosum, pedatum* and *tenellum*.

An important point in all fern cases is to have them so constructed as to be easily turned about and moved around, so that the plants may all share equally in the sunlight. If the case is too large, many plants will receive an undue proportion of the sunlight, while others will be totally deprived.

The Germans, who have a greater fondness and taste for *Window Gardening* than any other nation, have some very tasteful fancies in the way of Ferneries and Rockeries in the windows.

Fig. 44 will illustrate one of them projecting outward from the side of the house. The arch frame above is also on the outside. Looking at the rockery within rising up out of the aquarium, we find the following plants which do well in the constant evaporation of the water :

Adiantum tenerum, cuneatum, formosum ; Davallia, pixidata ; Gymnogramma Peruviana ; Lomaria spicant ; onychicum japonicum ; Pteris serrulata ; Selaginella calsia ; Selaginella, umbrosa, Africana serpens, and *Wildenorii,* with *Acorus gramineus folius fol var ; Sibthorpia Europæa ; Panicum variegatum ; Torrenia Asiatica ; Ficus stipularis ; Tradescantia zebrina ; Hoya bella,* and *Æschynanthus zebrinus*

We mention the plants particularly, as perhaps some one may be disposed to copy the designs literally. We know of no form of Window Gardening so exquisite as this. A climbing vine may be twined around the outside of the window casement. The water in the aquarium must be contained in a vessel with glass sides, so that all portions may be discernible to the eye.

Fig. 45 is another of the designs for Window Gardens, similar to those described in our second chapter. Now it is peculiarly suitable to hardy ferns, and such native plants as the Partridge vine, Mosses, Lycopodiums, etc.

Fig. 46 is known as the Pickard Plant Case; but we do not discover any special feature different from those constructed by Miss Maling. It contains the same metal box for the soil; but instead of having the glass sides and top stationary, all are movable, and easily put up or taken down. The glass sides all come in sheets, which fit each into a light frame of their own; yet any one of these may be removed from the other without disturbing the rest. The front can be taken out in an instant by lifting, or fixed back again in its place by a couple of hooks and eyes; in short each side has a frame of its own, and when all are shut up together they are held firmly by hooks and eyes at top and ends. The interior of this case is filled with Caladiums, Begonias, and other plants of colored foliage, as well as ferns. It is intended specially for a case of soft wooded plants, such as are usually grown in the pots of the greenhouse.

A very pretty fern case is that of Fig. 47, also in the possession of Shirley Hibberd. The base is a stone vase, with hollow interior; the foot is a frame of wood; inside the vase is a zinc pan, wherein the ferns are placed, and the frame of glass fits over the pan; a couple of doors furnish access to the interior

Fig. 70.—Wardian Case.

Fig. 71.—Wardian Case.

and open or are closed by a little button fastener. The size is as follows: Height of vase and glass, 5 feet 9 inches; width of vase, 2 feet; height of glass frame, 3 feet. In the top of the glass frame Mr. Hibberd suspended four half cocoanut shells, in which he planted some ferns; holes are cut in the bottom for drainage; and copper wire only used for hanging them. The contents are thus described by Mr. Hibberd in his Floral World : " This case contains at the present time two pretty climbing plants; one is the common Ivy of the British woods, *Hedera helix*; the other is *Lygodium scandens*, an elegant climbing fern. The palmlike fern in the centre is *Nephrolepis exaltata*—the finest fern in the world for a centre piece; both because of its character and also that it may be cut without spoiling it, if it happens to grow too tall. With it are examples of *Pteris cretica albo-lineata*, an elegant variegated fern; *Niphobolus lingua*—a hardy tonguelike fern; *Onychium Japonicum*, most delicately divided; *Pteris crenata, Lastrea glabella, Doodia caudata, Asplenium viride*, and some bits of *Selaginellas, Anemone nemorosa*, and a few *Mosses*.

The Ivy gained a footing quite by accident. This, with other of our cases, is frequently exhibited. On one occasion, in preparing some cases for a festive meeting, we introduced into this a number of little twigs of common Ivy among the ferns. The case was left undisturbed afterwards, and then on removing the Ivy one of them was found to have rooted. It was allowed to remain and it soon formed a rich shell on one side of the glass, without robbing a single fern of a ray of light. There it remains to this day; it is now some nine years old as an inhabitant of this case, and is as vigorous as ever. A few lengths of fine copper wire serve to train the Ivy and the *lygodium*, which add very much indeed to the beauty of this little garden. This case stands in the window, and has only the warmth of an ordinary room in winter.

For a fern case to stand in the sunshine all the time, and with a room of high temperature, choose the following tender ferns : In the centre place a fine plant of the *Cheilanthes farinosa*; then add here and there *Anemidictyon, phyllitidis, Olfersia cervina, Diplazium radicans, Asplenium fragrans, Lomaria attenuata, Pteris calomelanos, Fadyema prolifera*, and a few tufts of the *Selaginella caesium* and *S laevigata*."

Among fern decorations nothing is so striking, and yet so novel, as the fire brick. For filling a vacant fire place and making the screen appear ornamental, nothing is of better fitness. They are the invention of a physician, Dr. G. Churchill Watson, of Chester, England, and so constructed as to fit into the sides of walls of conservatories, ferneries and greenhouses, affording a convenient method of rendering a blank wall useful as well as ornamental. They are made of porous material, usually pottery, and round or oval shaped, with a concave centre, in which may be placed wet ferns, mosses or Lycopodiums. They are of different sizes, from $3\frac{1}{2}$ inches in diameter to 14 inches, and adapted to the place where they are most needed. The largest can be used to fit into the niche of an unused fire place, and the smaller ones can be used to fit the niches of a fern column or pillar. A fern pillar is one of the curiosities our parlor gardeners do not often behold; and yet a glance at illustration No. 48, will show how pleasing such a decoration might be, and how simply it could be made. This design is constructed of wood, in the form of a hexagonal pillar, with vase at the top.

At various places in each side are little niches or openings, into which are introduced the fern shells; these are filled with earth, usually holding a pint to a quart, and the fern grows gracefully outward. This pillar holds 19 vessels, and affords a rare opportunity of cultivating quite a variety. If the centre of the pillar is hollow it must be filled up by hand with some earthy material, and either moss or cocoanut fibre or dust may be pressed firmly. The soil for the bricks should be peat two parts; loam or woods mould one part, silver sand one part.

An English lady, filling such a case, once adopted this selection of plants. As mentioned in the Gardener's Magazine, "In the vase at the top were some plants of the *Asplenium flabellifolium*, one of the most elegant of all the small trailing ferns. To help out the effect of this, a tuft of the pretty rush *Isolepis gracilis* is introduced. This falls over in most graceful glass-like outlines, and as it loves moisture it is quite at home under a bell glass. In the shells at the sides of the column are specimens of *Adiantum eapillus veneris, A. hispidulums*, and *A. cuneatum*, the last of which may grow too large; if so, it should be removed. One of the most suitable of all ferns is *Woodsia Ilvensis*, which grows marvelously, and seems to be at home in the porous ware of the vessel. Other good ferns are *Asplenium fontanum, A. rutamuraria, Doodia lunulata, Doodia caudata, Woodsia obtusa, Cystopteris fragile Dickeana, Camptozaurus, rhizophyllus,* (one of the rarest of the exotic Hearts Tongue ferns,) *Scolopendrium vulgare, v. proliferum vamo marginatum,* and *v. polyschides, Lastrea filix-mas v. Schofieldii, Adiantum setulosum, Hymenophyllum Wilsoni, Athyrium f. f. diffissum.*

These are the cheapest of all designs for the window. Fig. 59 and 60 being obtainable at almost any glass store, at prices of $2.00 to $5.00 complete. Figs. 61 and 62, are in a basket vase. Figs. 63 and 64 are with pottery ware or lava boxes, resting upon stands. Fig. 65, is made of rustic wood and has a wooden bowl, upon which the glass cylinder rests. Fig. 66 is an iron stand, with a plain earthen bowl beneath the fernery, the outside of which is decorated with a network of wire.

Among the various designs of Wardian Cases, for the drawing-room or saloon, there are often met a few of much simpler material, which can be used for other purposes. Figs. 67 and 68 are so constructed that they can be used at one time for growing ferns within, or they can be used merely for holding cut flowers in moist sand or water. In Fig. 68, the top is movable, fitting into a brass groove, and must be lifted entirely off the table when the plants are to be placed inside or need any attention. All the ornamental work around the edges of the stand, and the frame work for holding the glass plates, is made of brass; the stand itself is of wood. The size of the interior is about 18 inches in diameter, by 12 inches high.

Fig. 67 is much more symmetrical in shape, and easily made. The frame of this, too, is made mostly of polished brass, and the glass sets down upon a groove made in the top of the stand, which is of wood. The interior is hollow, with a zinc basin for holding plants.

Fig. 69 is a *Lady's Plant Case*, a kind of Wardian case in miniature; and though not affording very spacious accommodations inside, still there is a good deal of novelty in its construction, sufficient to render it a very interesting object for either the drawing room or library.

A bell glass, or shade, fits closely at its base into a groove running all around the edge of a stand constructed usually of wood.

The plants inside are in small pots not over four inches in diameter, although the proportions of the case may be enlarged from 18 inches in diameter up to 3 feet, and afford greater room. Any manufacturer of glass shades could make such a shade in a special mould, and any cabinet maker could fashion a tasteful table or stand beneath.

Figs. 71, 72 are sketches of two very pretty Wardian Cases, exhibited at one of the Horticultural Society Exhibitions, and was much admired. They admit of considerably greater outline than the previous designs of Ferneries, and are more ornamental. Fig. 70 is 7 feet high, 4 feet 2 inches wide, and 2 feet 6 inches in breadth.

Fig. 71 is 4 feet high, 3 feet broad, and 1 foot 11 inches wide. These are constructed mostly with bright metallic frame work; the best quality of sheet glass is used; castors are fitted to the base, and at the back there is a little door to allow the entrance of the hand for watering the plants or removing dead leaves.

Such designs as these, made to cover an entire collection of plants, should be generally adopted, and their manufacture encouraged. They do away altogether with the daily task of watering, they are absolutely free from dust, and the plants have a perpetual moisture inside, which affords not only the most desirable and uniform temperature, but conduces to health of habit, and freedom from insects. Our Window Gardeners must learn by practical experience that there is but one practical solution to the difficulties of Window Gardening, "*The plants must live in an atmosphere to themselves, shut out alike from the air of the room, and from the outer air.*"

In apartments lighted with gas, the use of these glass covers or shades is again made obvious, for no gas fumes will ever touch them.

An opinion is general among amateurs, that these Wardian Cases must be perfectly air tight. This is not quite true; although they are fitted pretty close, yet they are not absolutely air tight. Indeed it is sometimes quite desirable that the case should be lifted a little to permit a free circulation of the air betwixt the interior and the exterior, especially if there is a surplus of moisture inside, and condenses so constantly upon the glass that the plant cannot be seen.

A fact may often have been observed by flower lovers, that when two flowers are plucked, the one stuck with its stem into a bottle or vase of water, and the other thrown down into a wide basin of water, so the petals as well as stem are in the

WINDOW GARDENING.

water, it will be found that the latter will keep fresh and sweet the longest. The explanation is only in the greater humidity. In the former case, the air of the room being too dry, evaporates the water from the surface of the petals faster than the stem can supply, while in the latter the flower is completely surrounded with all it needs.

Observing this principle then in your cut flowers or bouquets, if you will take care to place them in pans of water, or sand and water, and then cover with bell glasses, they will have a humid atmosphere entirely to themselves, retain their freshness for double the length of time, as they would if exposed to the dry air of the sitting-room.

The Wardian Case then, in principle, is not only the most practical in operation, but beneficial in results.

List of Ferns.

For a Wardian Case kept in a room with a high temperature, use:

Adiantum *cuneatum, tenerum, *formosum, trapeziforme, Veitchii, rubellum, concinnum, Farleyense.
Anemia *hirta, flexuosa, villosa.
*Asplenium viviparum.
Blechnum *brasiliense, Corcovadense.
Cheilanthes Alabamensis, Borsigiana, hirta, microphylla, pulveracea, spectabilis.
Davallia *decora, *Mooreana, *polyantha.
Didymochlaena lunulata.
Doryopteris nobilis, *pedata.
Gymnogramma *tartarea, *chrysophylla, Laurheana, Peruviana.

Hemionites *palmata.
Microlepia Davallia, hirsuta-angusta.
Nephrolepis *exaltata, *pectinata.
Nothoclaena chrysophylla, *nivea, tenera.
Polypodium aureum, omyxifolium.
Pteris * falcata, tricolor.

Selaginella.

Selaginella caesia arborea, *Africana, atrovirens, caulescens. *conferta, Lyallii, *umbrosa (erythropus), Kasleniana, *serpens, *imbricaulis, Wallichii, Warcswewitzii.

The above Ferns and Selaginellas are also suitable for general decorations in a well heated room. Such marked * are useful for the window without glass covering.

2. For a Wardian Case in a moderately heated room:

Acrostichum *alcicorne (Platicerium.)
Adiantum affine, *capillus Veneris, assimile, *colpodes, *formosum, *rubellnm, reniforme.
Asplenium *palmatnm, Fabianum
Blechnum *australe, Cyathea medullaris, australis.
Cyrtomium *falcatum.
Davallia *canariensis, *pixidata.
Dicksonia *antarctica.

Lygodium scandens, palmatum.
Asplenium nidus, avis.
Aspidium *molle, *violascens, *Kaulfussie.
Nephrolepis *exaltata, *tuberosa.
Nothoclaena trichomanoides.
Oleandra *neriifolia.
Onychium *japonicum.
Pteris *arguta, argyraea, *cretica alba, *serrulata * falcata, longifolia.

Doodia aspera, caudata, *rupestris.
Doryopteris *palmata.
Drynaria coronans.
Lastraea glabella.
Lomaria *gibba.

Woodwardia radicans
Selaginella apoda, *caesia, *denticulata, stolonifera, formosa, involvens, Sohottii, *Martensii albo var, *Wildenowii

The above named Ferns and Lycopodias are also suitable for general decorations in a moderately heated room. Those marked * are useful for the window.

3. For a cold room, open hall, veranda, rockwork, or for cool shaded places near the building:

Adiantum pedatum.
Allosorus crispus.
Aspidium goldianum.
Asplenium septentrionale, fontanum, trichomanes, ruta-muraria, viride.
Aathyrium felix foemina, gracile, multiceps.
Blechnum boreale, occidentale.
Ceterach officinarum.
Cystopteris montana.
Lastraea oreopteris, dilatata, filix-mas, rigida.

Onoclea sensibilis.
Osmunda regalis, cinnamomea.
Polypodium vulgare.
Polystichium angulare, lonchitis, Scolopendrium officinarum and varieties.
Struthiopteris germanica.
Pteris aquilina.
Woodsia hyperborea, ilvensis.
Lycopodium clavatum, alpinum, selago, dendroideum.

The above named Ferns and Lycopodia are also suitable for window decoration during the summer season, but require some shade.

LADIES' FANCY WORK.

A Charming New Book, with above title. A Companion Volume to

Household Elegancies

And WINDOW GARDENING.

Being issued in same size and style, profusely illustrated with engravings of superior execution, and devoted to many topics of Household Taste, Fancy Work for the ladies, and containing hundreds of suggestions of Home Decoration.

IT WILL CONSTITUTE VOLUME 3
—OF—
Williams' Household Series.

CONTENTS.

Among the topics which "Ladies' Fancy Work" will treat of, are,—

Feather Work, Paper Flowers, Fire Screens, Shrines, Rustic Pictures, a charming series of designs for Easter Crosses, Straw Ornaments, Shell Flowers and Shell work, Bead Mosaic, and Fish Scale Embroidery, Hair Work, Cardboard Ornaments, Fancy Rubber Work, Cottage Foot Rests, Window Garden Decorations, Illuminating, Grecian and Oriental Painting, Crochet Work, Modeling in Clay and Plaster, Fret-Work, Wood Carving, designs in Embroidery, and an immense number of designs of other Fancy Work to delight all lovers of Household Art and Recreations.

The volume will be fully equal in elegance to the volumes of the HOUSEHOLD SERIES, already issued, and in variety of topics, and abundance of engravings, will probably be in many respects superior in interest.

SPECIAL NOTICE.

Any individual, a member of the trade, desiring advance copies of "LADIES' FANCY WORK," when ready, may forward to me their names for record, and I will forward to them a Circular of Announcement, with full description of Contents, price and exact date for delivery, by mail or to the book trade.

Price $1.50.
ADAMS & BISHOP,
PUBLISHERS.
46 Beekman Street, N. Y.

Household Elegancies,

THE MOST BEAUTIFUL LADIES' BOOK EVER PUBLISHED.

A BEAUTIFUL GIFT TO FRIENDS.

By Henry T. Williams and Mrs. C. S. Jones.

A splendid new book on Household Art, devoted to a multitude of topics, interesting to ladies everywhere. Among the most popular subjects are, Transparencies on Glass, Leaf Work, Autumn Leaves, Wax Work, Painting, Leather Work, Fret Work, Picture Frames, Brackets, Wall Pockets, Work Boxes and Baskets, Straw Work, Skeleton Leaves, Hair Work, Shell Work, Mosaic, Crosses, Cardboard Work, Worsted Work, Spatter Work, Mosses, Cone Work, etc. Hundreds of exquisite illustrations decorate the pages, which are full to overflowing with hints and devices to every lady, how to ornament her home cheaply, tastefully and delightfully, with fancy articles of her own construction. By far the most popular and elegant gift-book of the year.—300 pages, Price, $1.50. Sent post-paid by mail.

Address, ADAMS & BISHOP, Publishers, 46 Beekman Street, New York.